AF268884

Still Forms

Michael Sohn

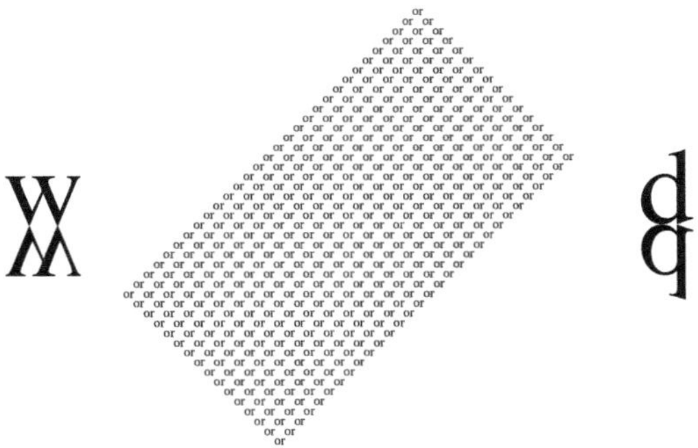

Visible Poetry

Wet Cement Press
Berkeley, California

ISBN: 978-1-7324369-7-8

Wet Cement Press
Berkeley, California
www.wetcementpress.com

Cover image: Michael Sohn

Acknowledgments:
Since this book was a long time coming into being, I have quite a few people to thank. John High for the decade long continuing conversation. Benjamin Egnatz who has read and commented on my poetry for over 20 years. Wayne Berninger who first published many of these poems in Downtown Brooklyn, the literary journal of Long Island University Brooklyn. Bill and Judy Plott who are responsible for many things. Tom Puchalsky who would be incensed. Richard Sieburth who would be pleased. Barbara Katz and Joel Owen for their years of service. My mother and father. And Thoreau Lovell for such a lovely book.

WCP6-3

Contents

For Ann

pour m'avoir introduit dans ton histoire

Disquiet

That is how I am. When I want to think, I look.

—Bernardo Soares (Fernando Pessoa), *The Book of Disquiet*

I

Thinking

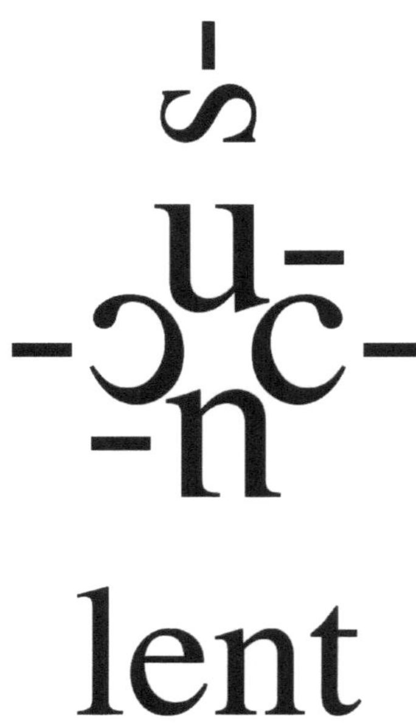

heist

erst-
while a
wile
                a-

way a-
while

gist

(adjacent)

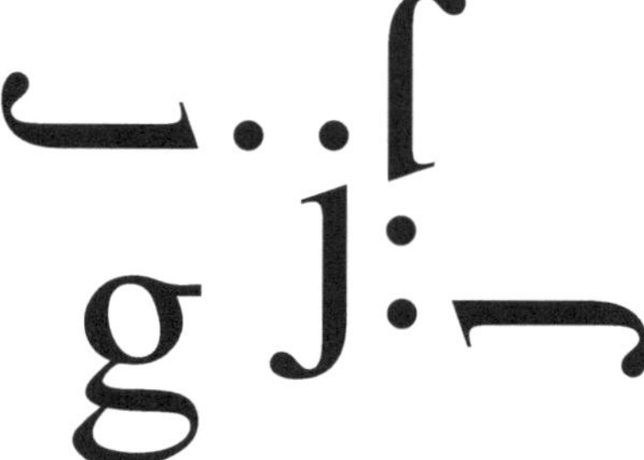

lent : late

lathe

let the
rest

rowse
a

worse
ruse

teal : tale

furor for or

vastation

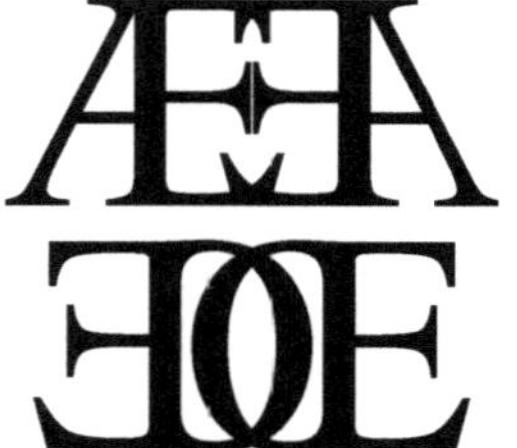

œ

æ

II

Looking

succulent succulent succulent succulent

erst-
while a
wile
a--a

way a-
while

erst-
while a
wile
a--a

way a-
while

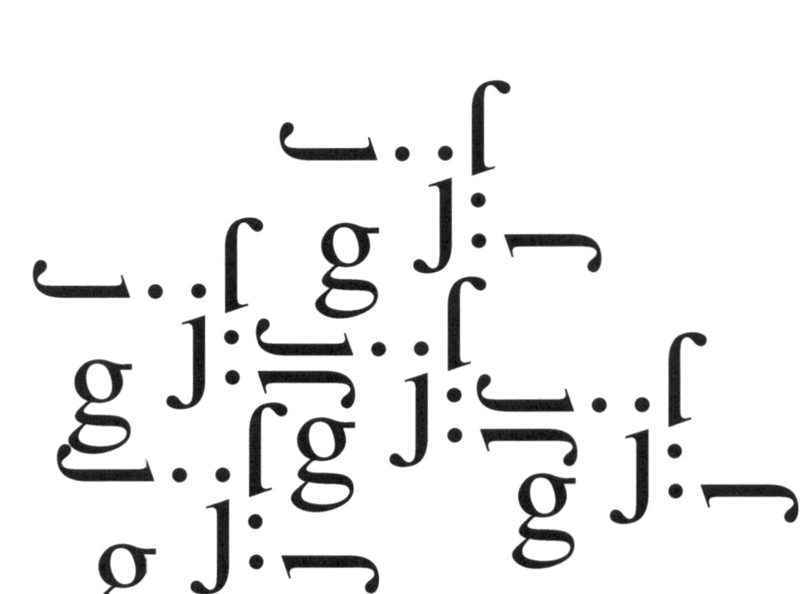

t h i s

i s h t

lent : late
lathe
let the
rest
rowse
a
worse
ruse
teal : tale

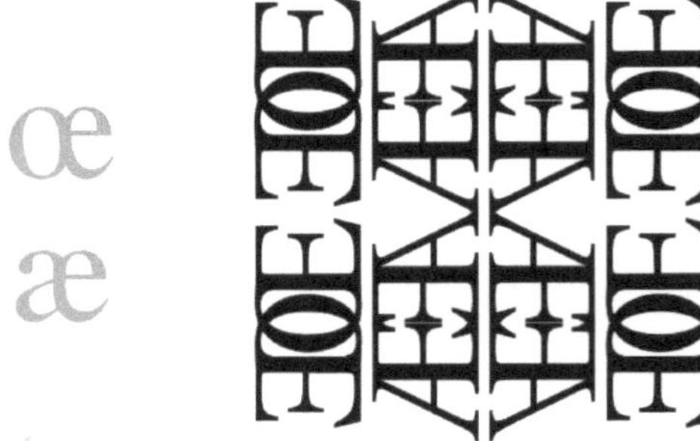

After Mira Schendel

For Mira Schendel

São Paul Biennial, September 1969: this is an attempt to show that the "other side" of transparency is in its front and that the "other world" is this one.

I

Monotipias
[Monotypes]

The [Monotipias] are the result of a hitherto frustrated attempt to capture dis-
course at its moment of origin. What concerns me is capturing the passage of
immediate experience, in all its empirical force, into the symbol, with its mem-
orability and relative immortality.

sumptuous

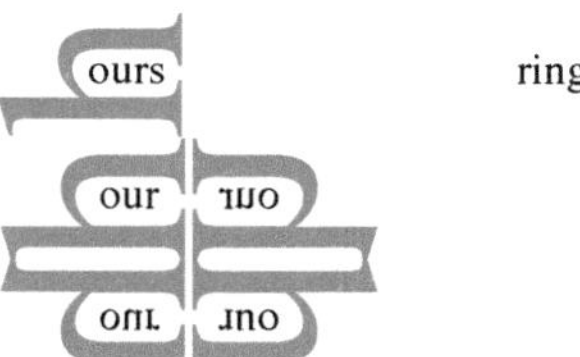

ring

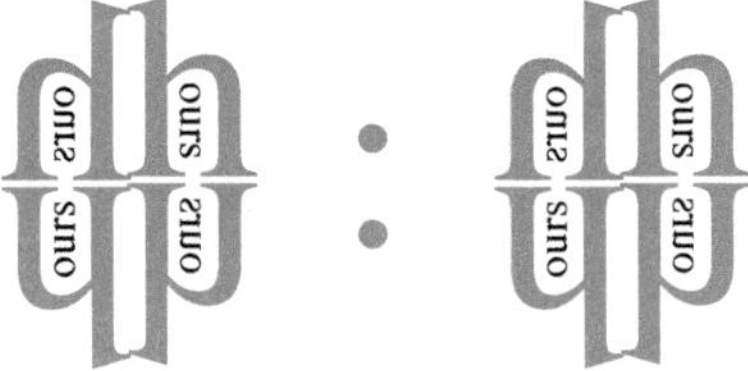

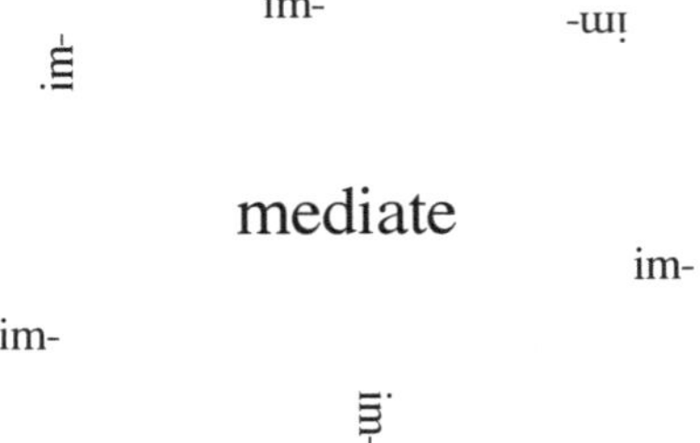

im-
im-
im-
mediate
im-
im-
im-

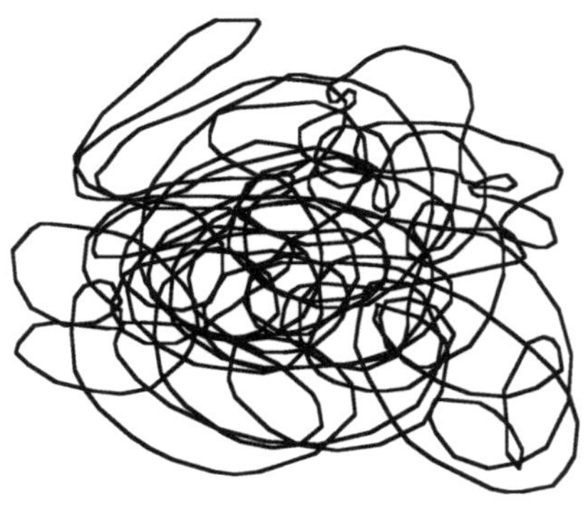

II

Droguihnas
[Little Nothings]

But that was an experiment, the *Droguinha*...a transitory object, something exposed to the world, to the elements, to dust, like our own lives.

paltry
try

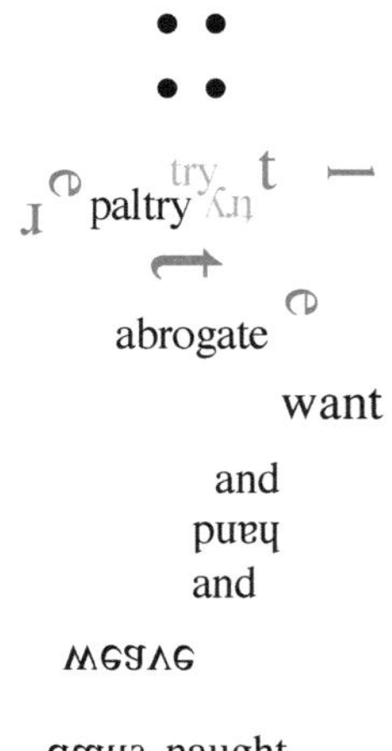

t

abrogate

want

and

hand

and

weave

naught
ephemeral

and hand
and   want   abrogate   weave 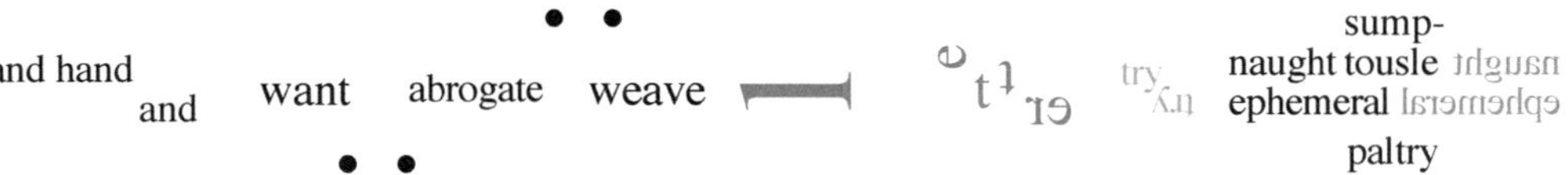   e t¹ er   try   sump-
                                                                                          naught tousle   naught
                                                                                          ephemeral ephemeral
                                                                                          paltry

and hand weave
want   and

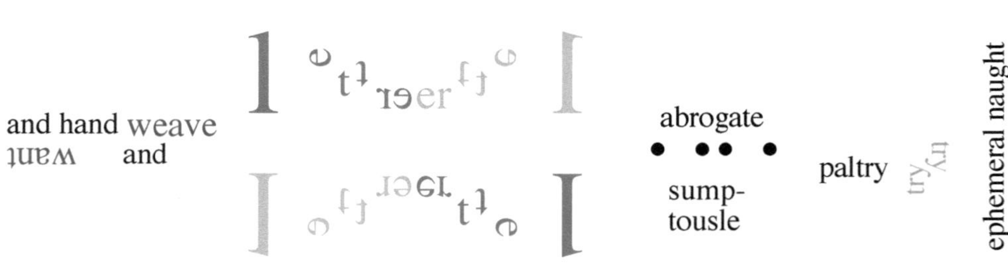

abrogate

sump-
tousle

paltry

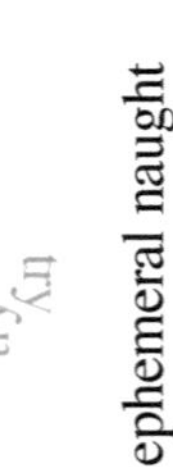

weave
want

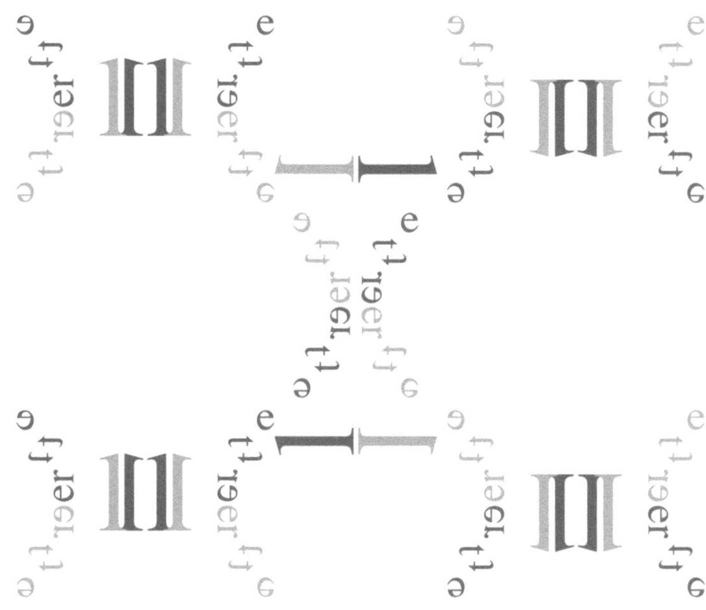

want
weave

III

Objectos Gráficos
[*Graphic Objects*]

That's where the large plates came from, the so-called *Objectos Gráficos*, which were an attempt to bring about drawing through transparency—in other words, to avoid back and front.

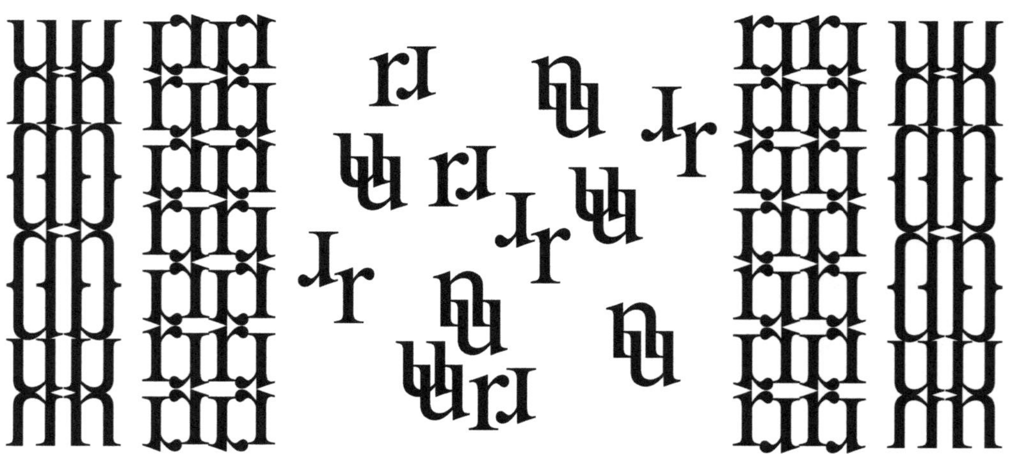

through

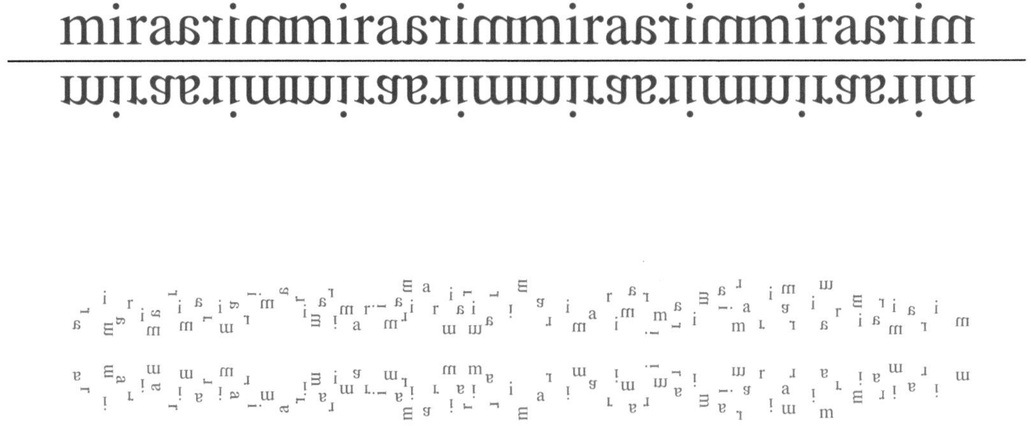

mirasrimmirasrimmirasrimmirasrim

After *TILA (Doors)*

for Pertti Kekarainen

Je ressens alors l'agréable et difficle faiblesse de notre écriture — ce aussi avec quoi il faut se battre et se ruser — qui rêve toujours de pictogrammes, d'idéogrammes, qui voudrait entretenir cette veine, si mince chez nous, qui fait du geste une écriture et de toute écriture la manifestation d'une présence corporelle.

—Nicolas Pesquès, *La face nord de Juliau, deux*

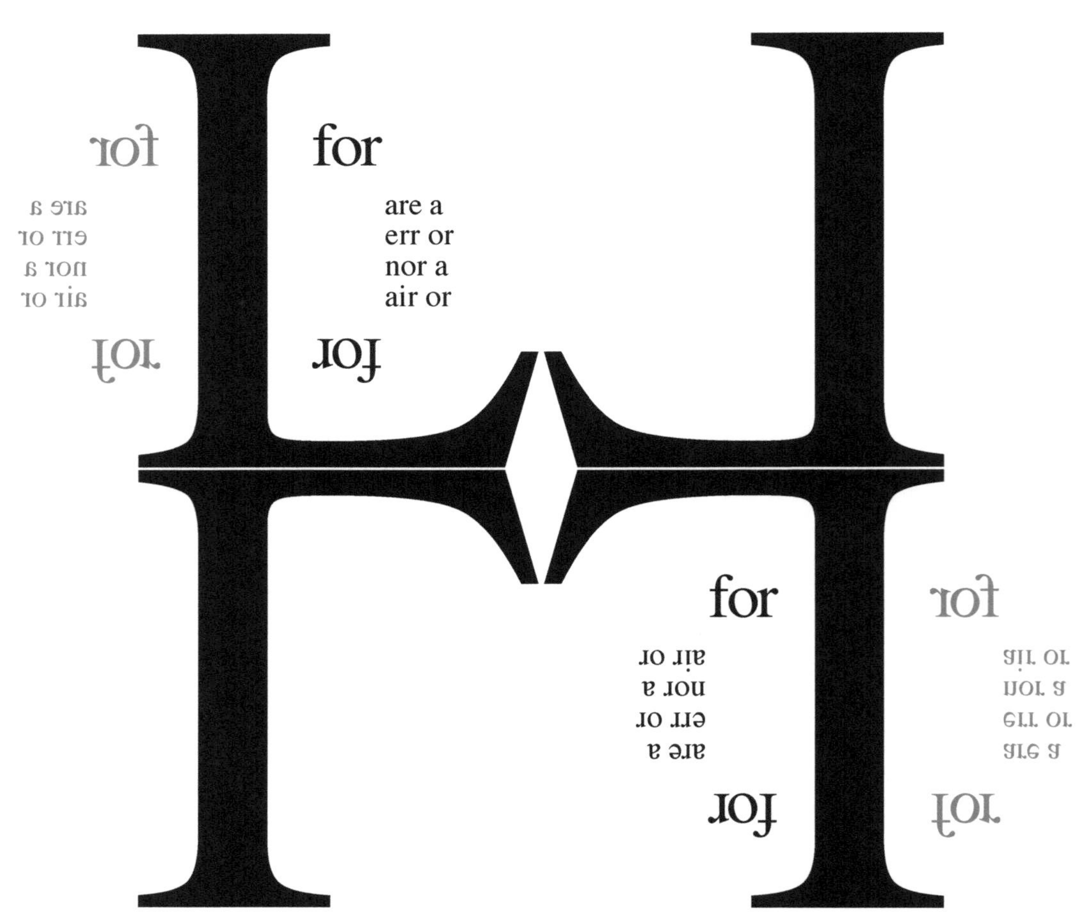
for
are a
err or
nor a
air or
for
for
are a
err or
nor a
air or
for

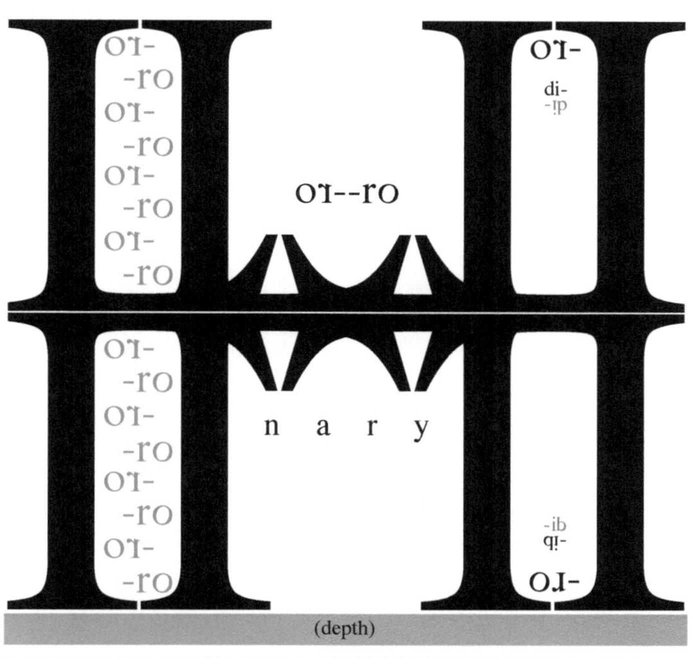
or--ro
nary
ordi-
(depth)
(debt)
depth

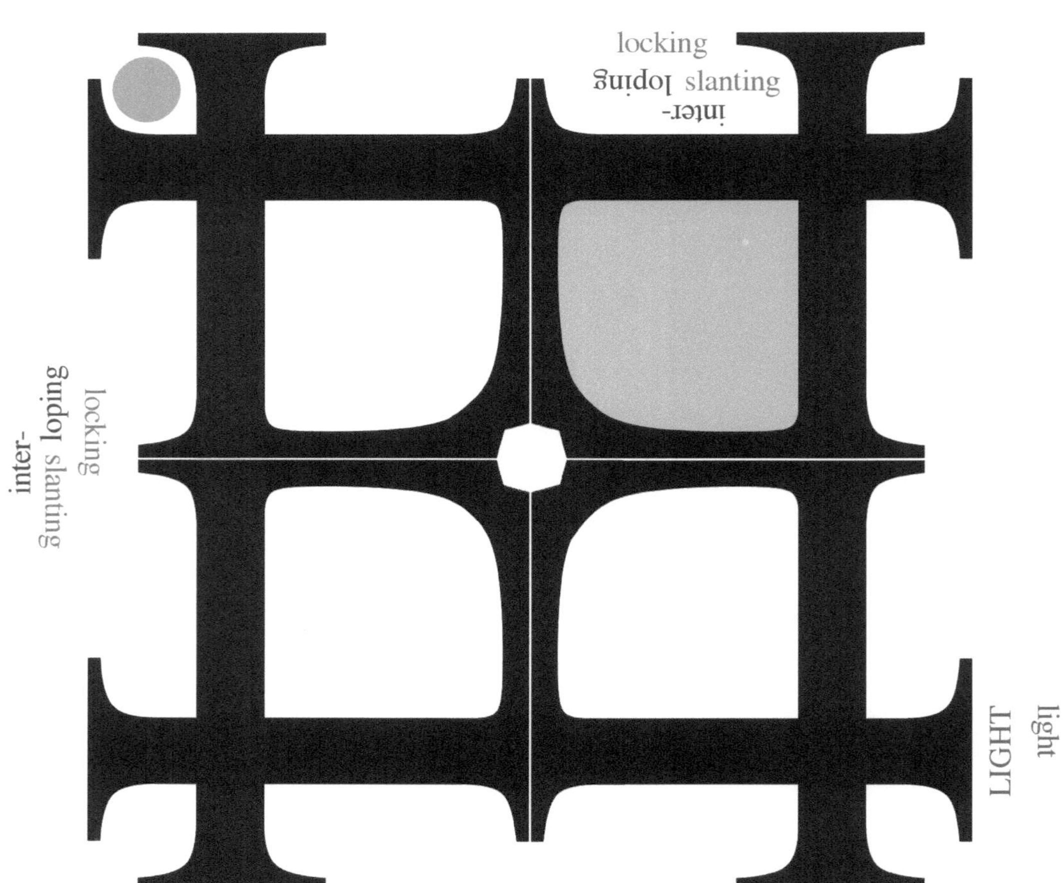
locking
inter-
loping slanting
locking
inter-
loping slanting
light
LIGHT

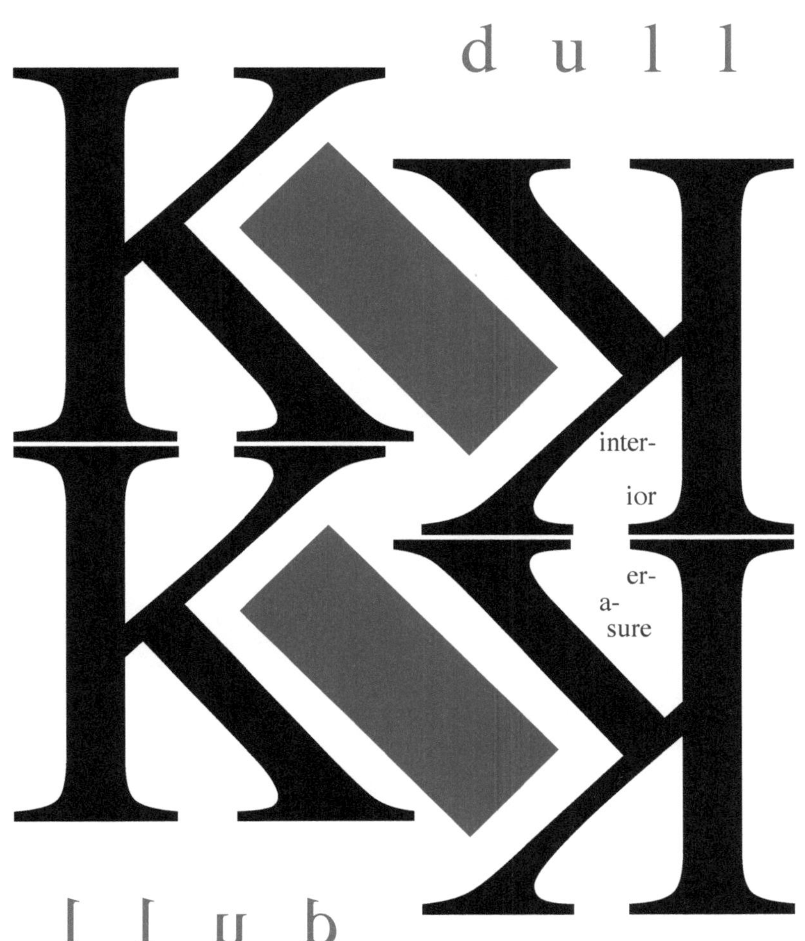
dull
inter-
ior
er-
a-
sure
dull

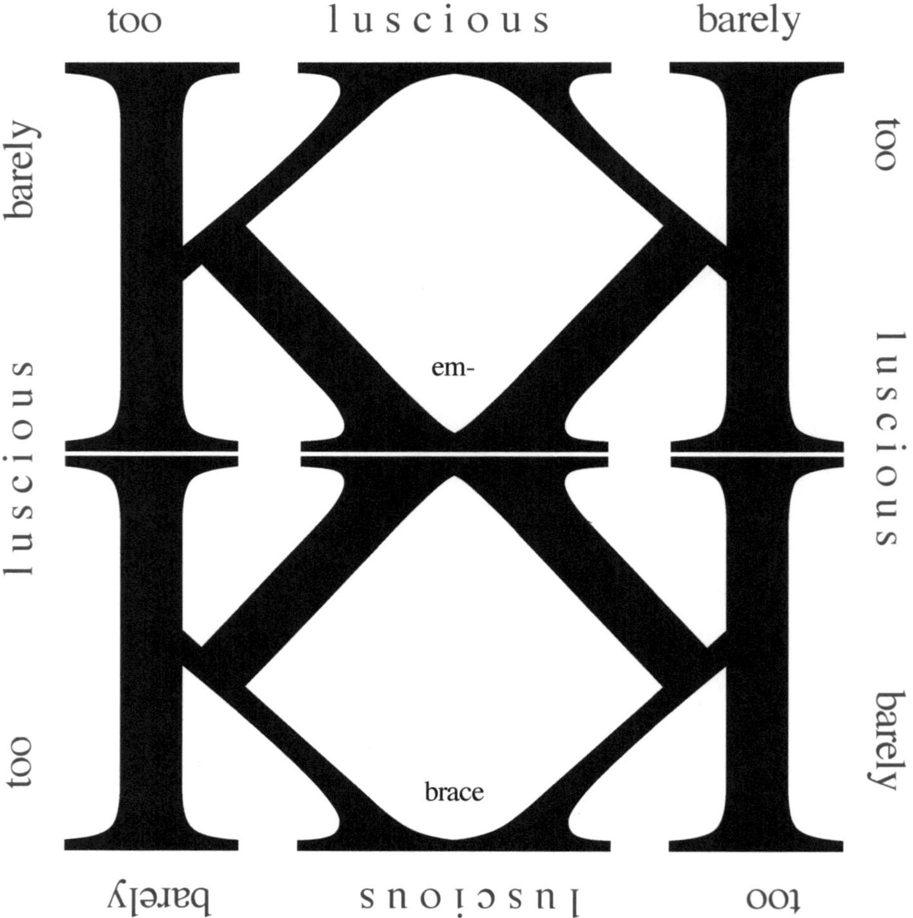

too
luscious
barely
too
barely
luscious
em-
brace
too
barely
barely
too
luscious
luscious

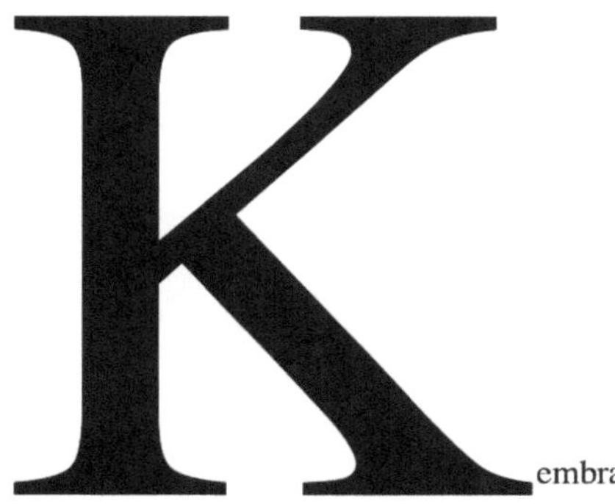

embrasure

cinnabar
sienna russet
icterine
sepia ochre
amaranth
ecru
bole
malachite alizarin aureolin
feldgrau
ceil
fulvous grullo
gamboge
cordovan
vermillion

PLINTH

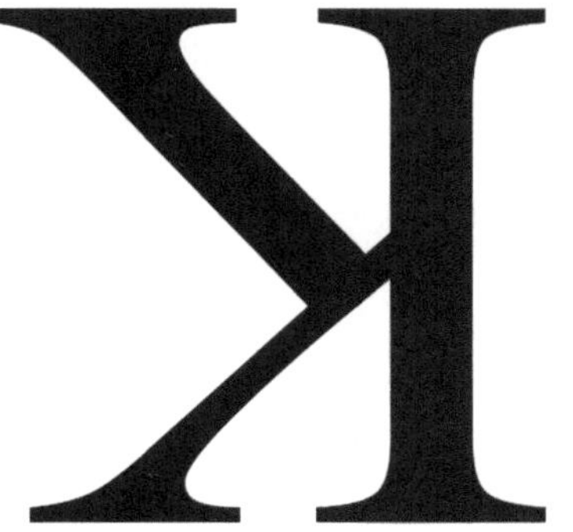

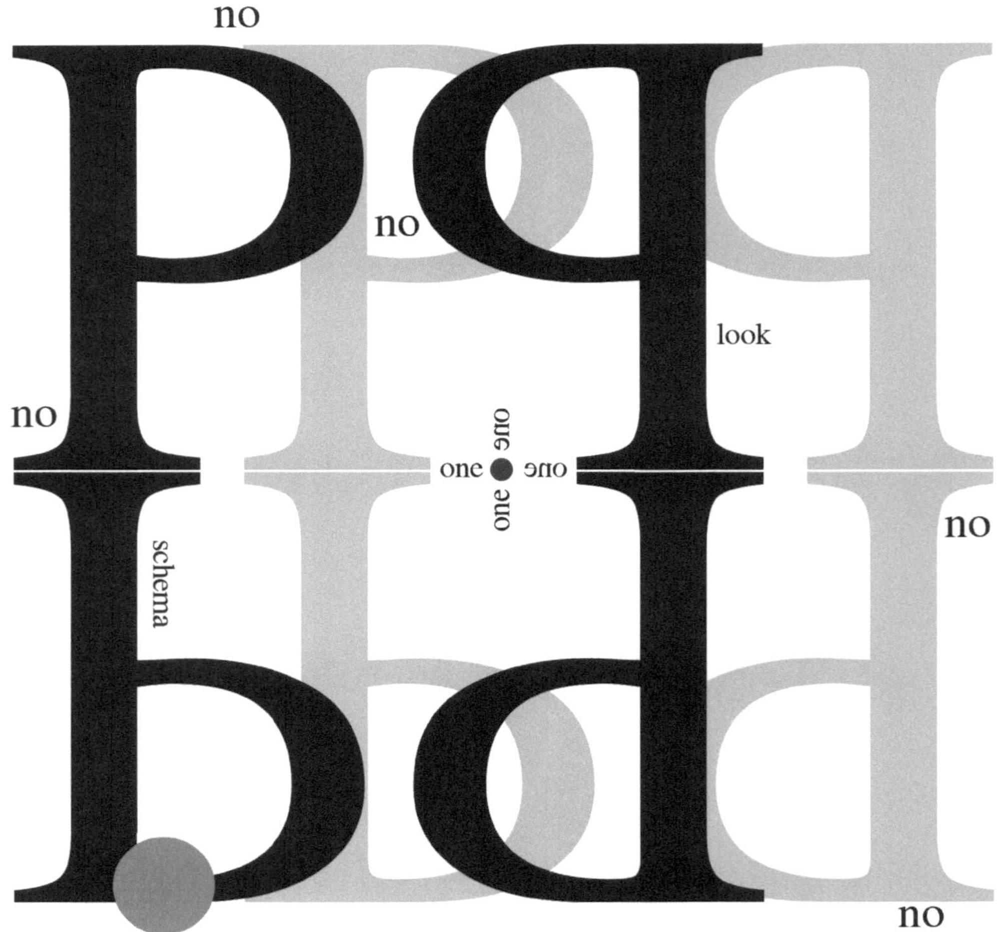

no
no
look
no
one
one
one one
one
no
schema
no
no

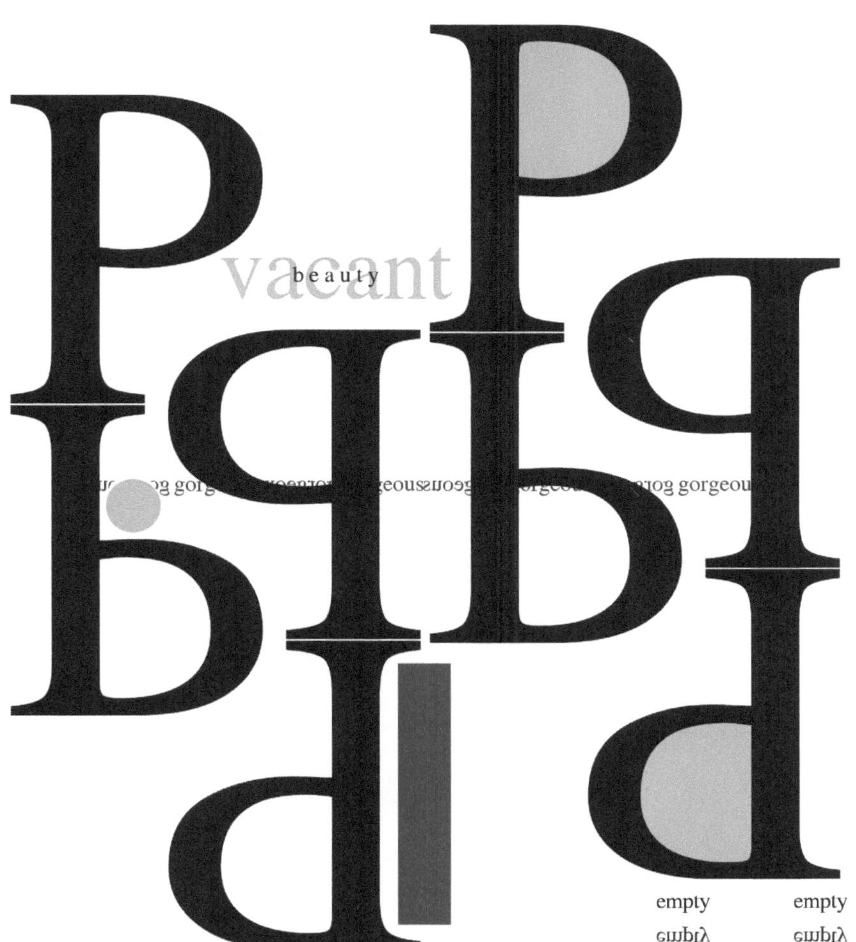

vacant
beauty
gorgeous
empty
empty

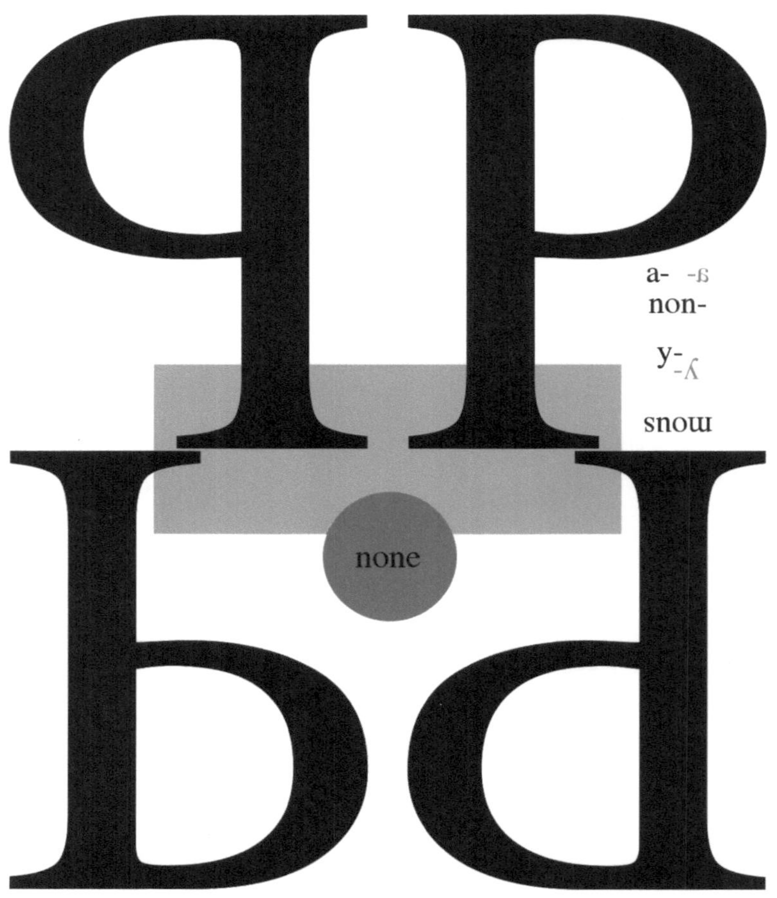
a-
non-
y-
mous
none
(name adj-
acent)

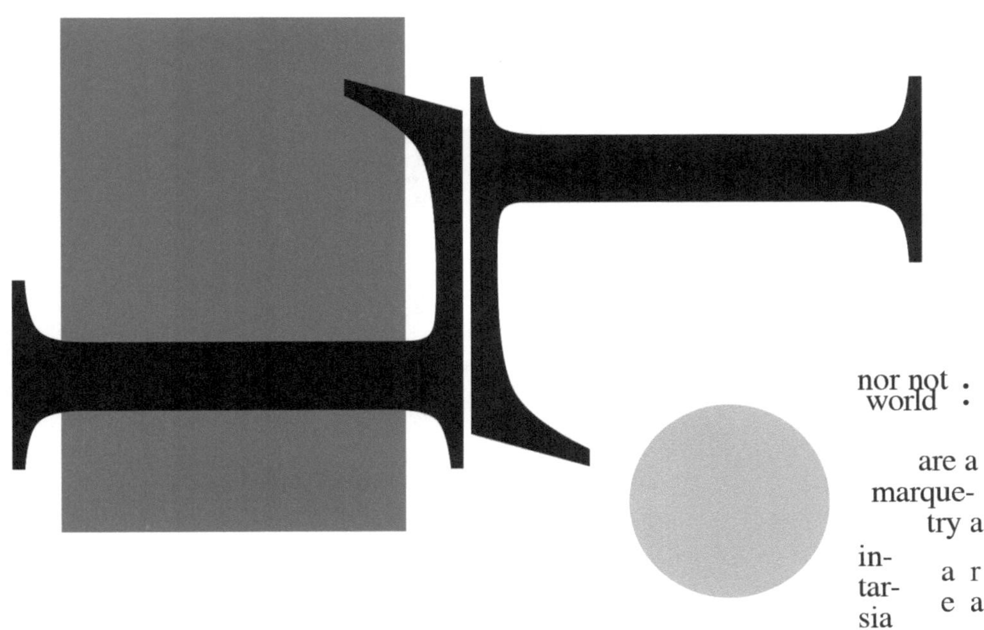

nor not
world :

are a
marque-
try a
in-   a   r
tar-   e   a
sia

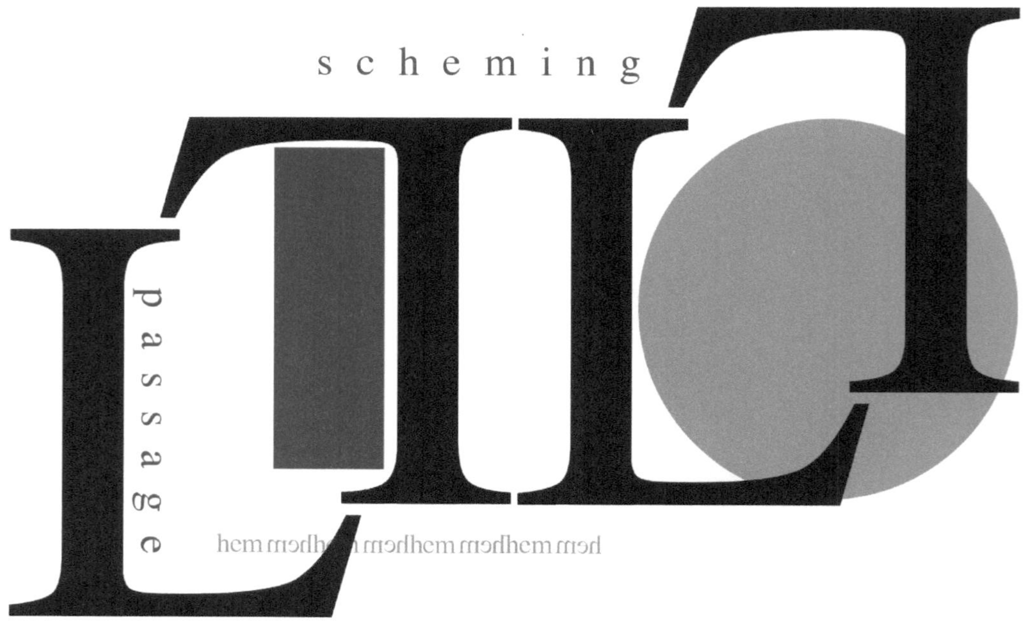

scheming
passage
hem methem methem methem methem meth

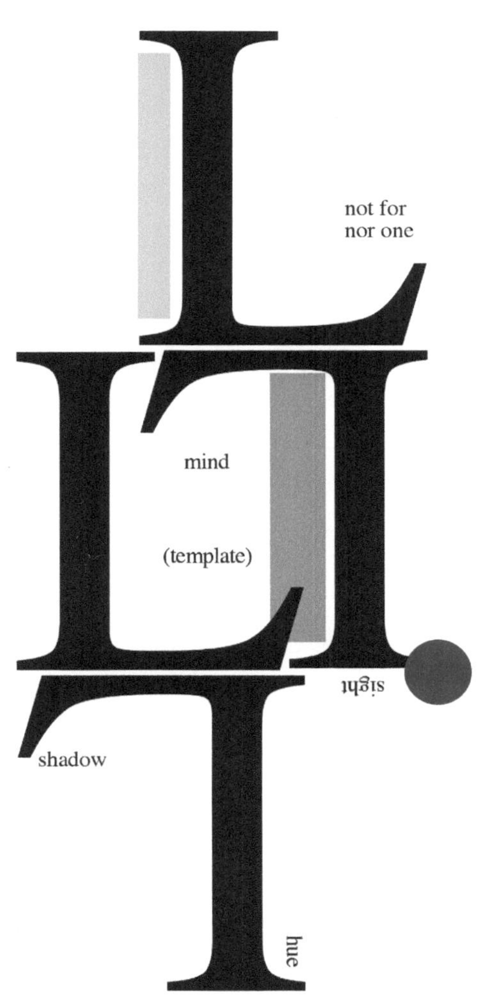

not for
nor one
mind
(template)
sight
shadow
hue

Même si je songe parfois à une écriture si extrême qu'elle puisse se passer de moi, des mots et de la chose. Gravitation du poème dans l'anonymat d'un sens lavé des scories d'un vocable, de la trace d'une chair et de l'anecdote d'un objet [...].

—Nicolas Pesquès, *La face nord de Juliau, deux*

After *Ken Price Sculpture: A Retrospective*

For Ken Price

I

Cup Constructions

The cup essentially presents a set of formal restrictions—sort of a preordained structure. The cup is its own subject, basically. It doesn't have to be about anything other than itself. But it can be used as a vehicle for ideas.

—Ken Price

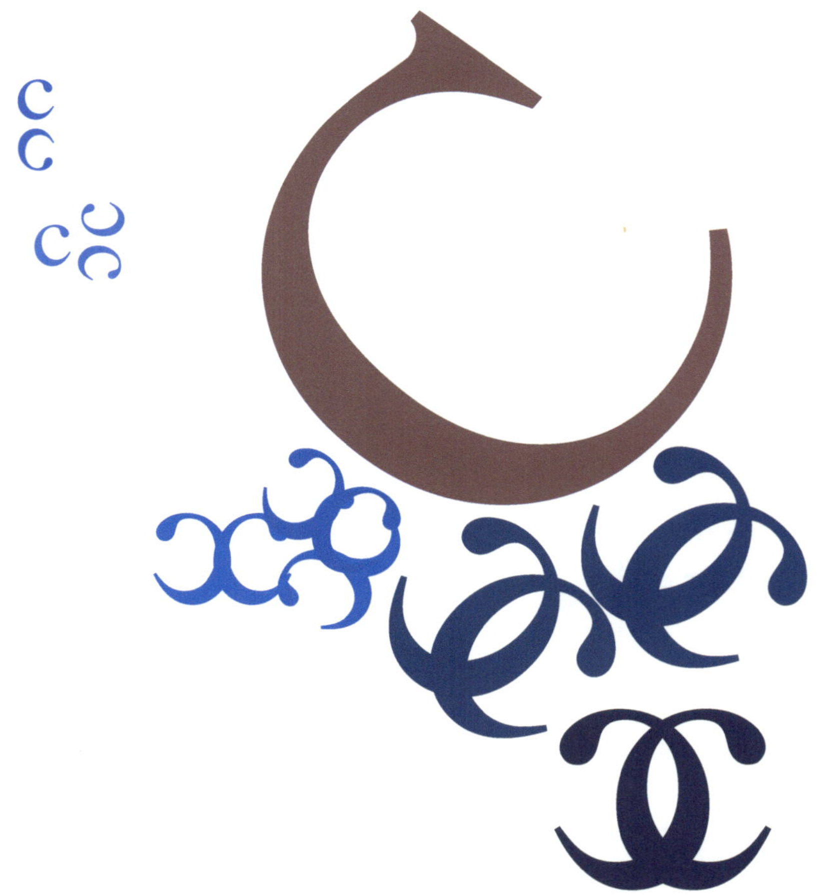

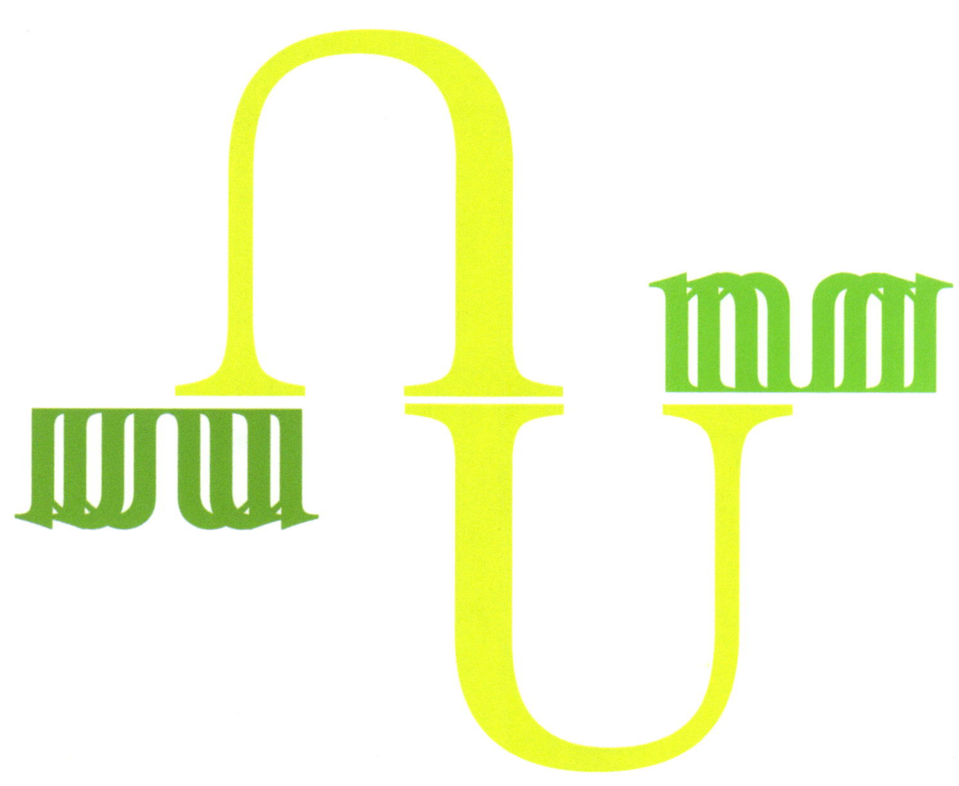

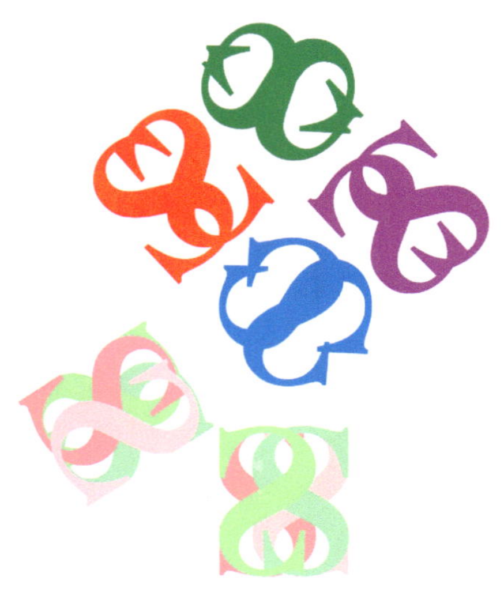
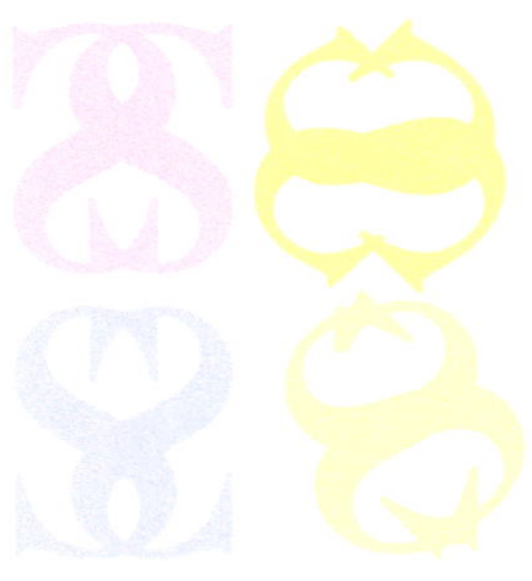

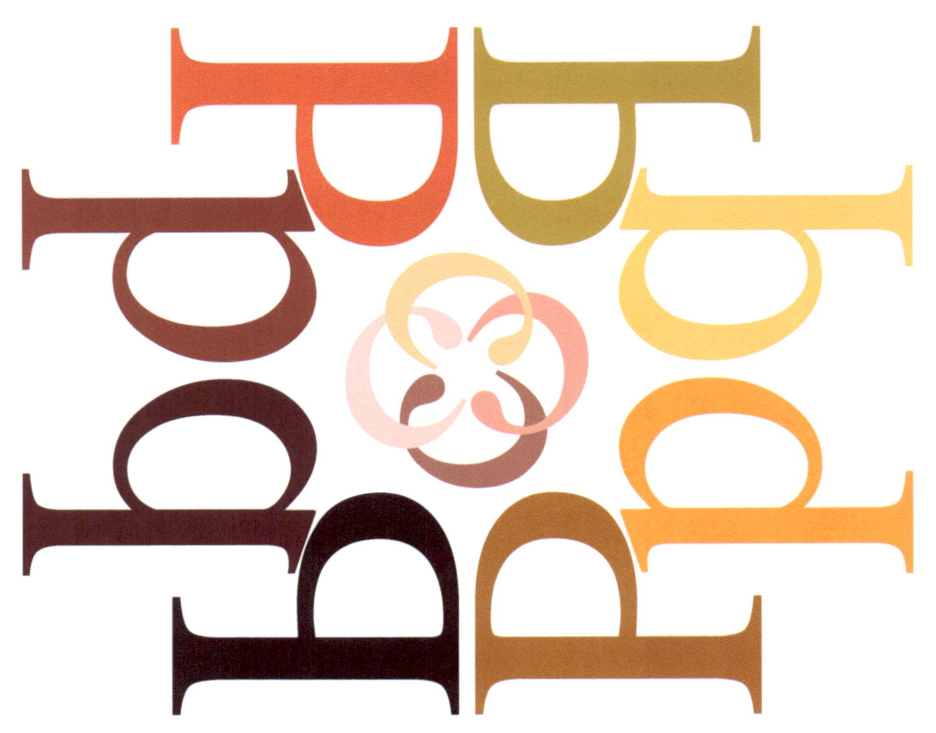

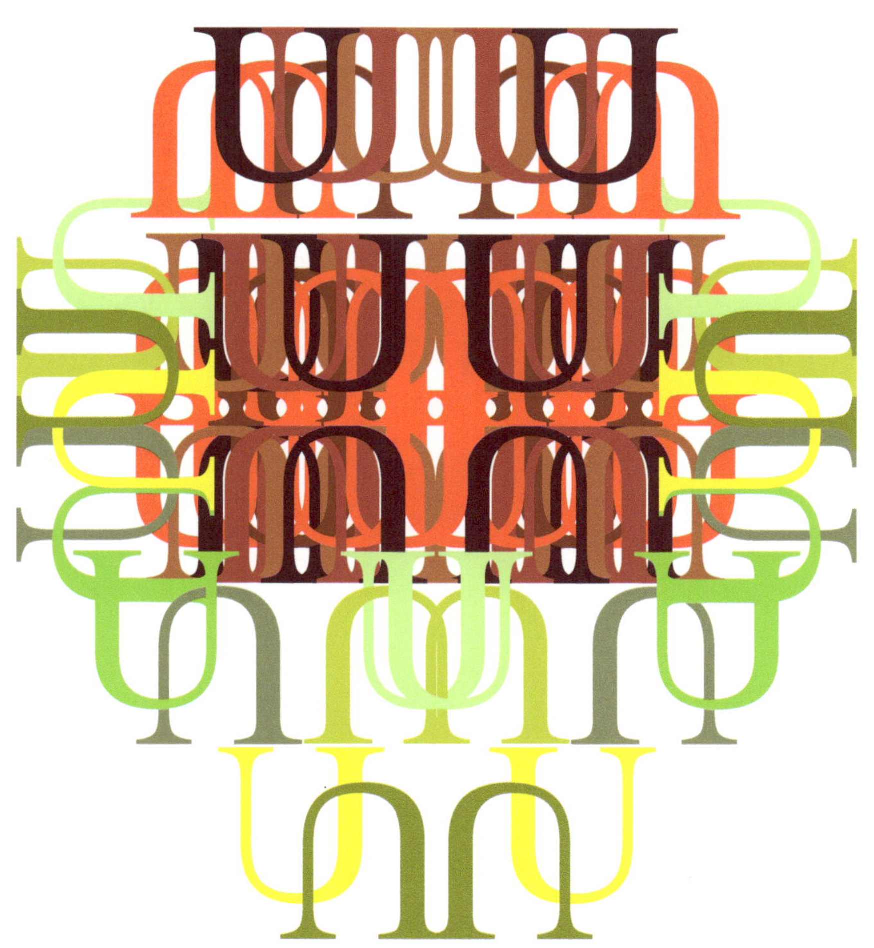

II

Slumps and Odd Forms

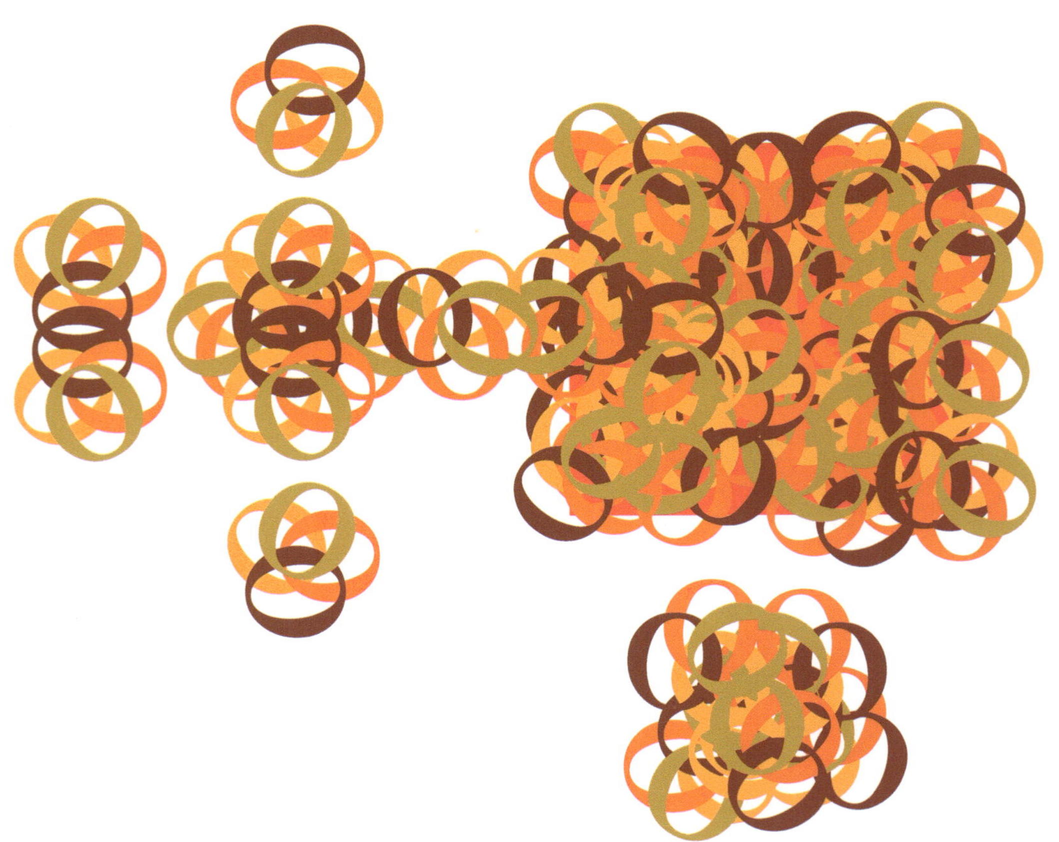

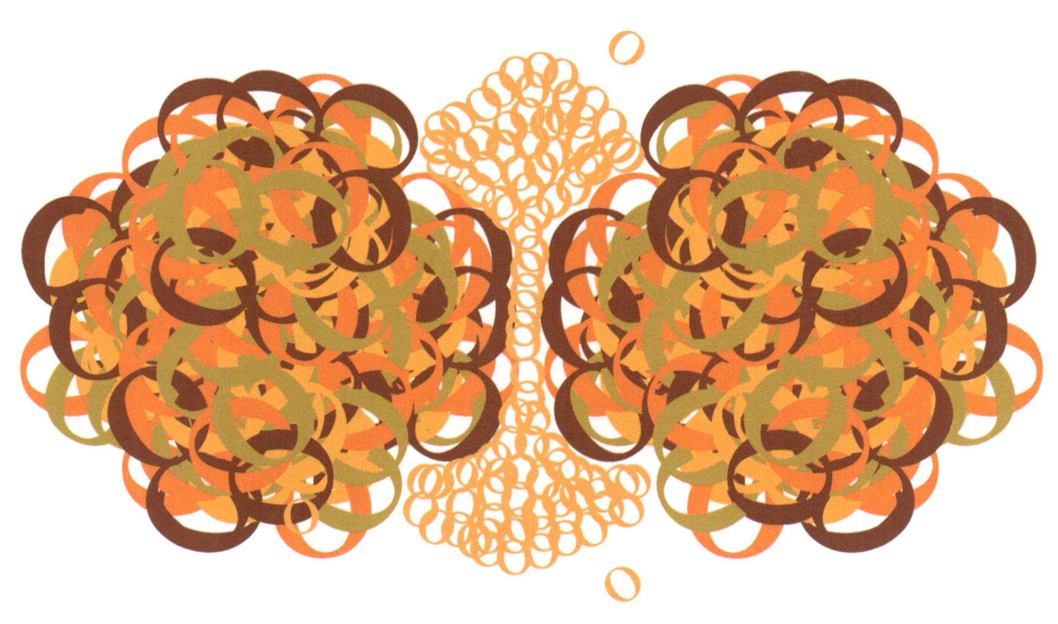

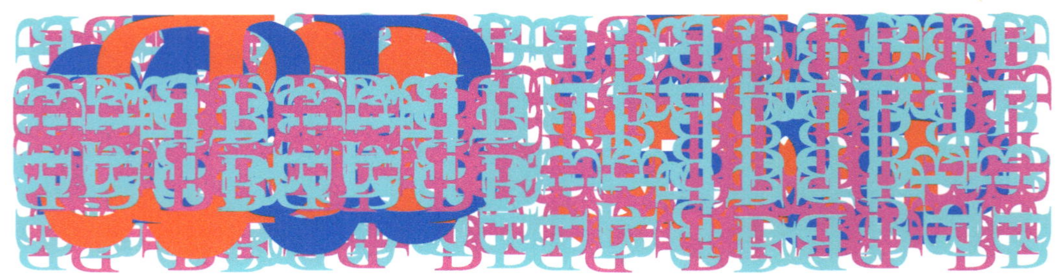
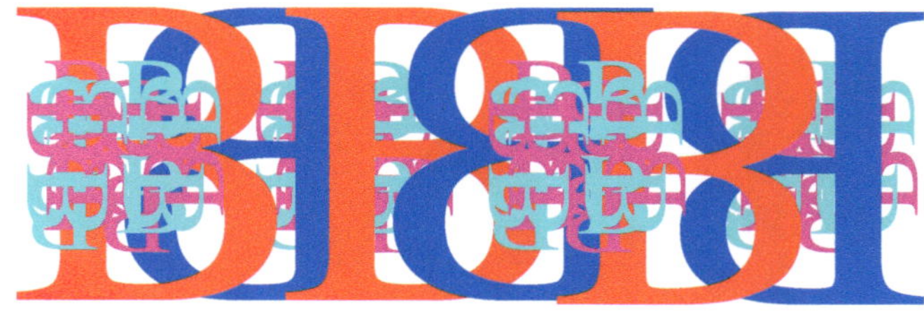

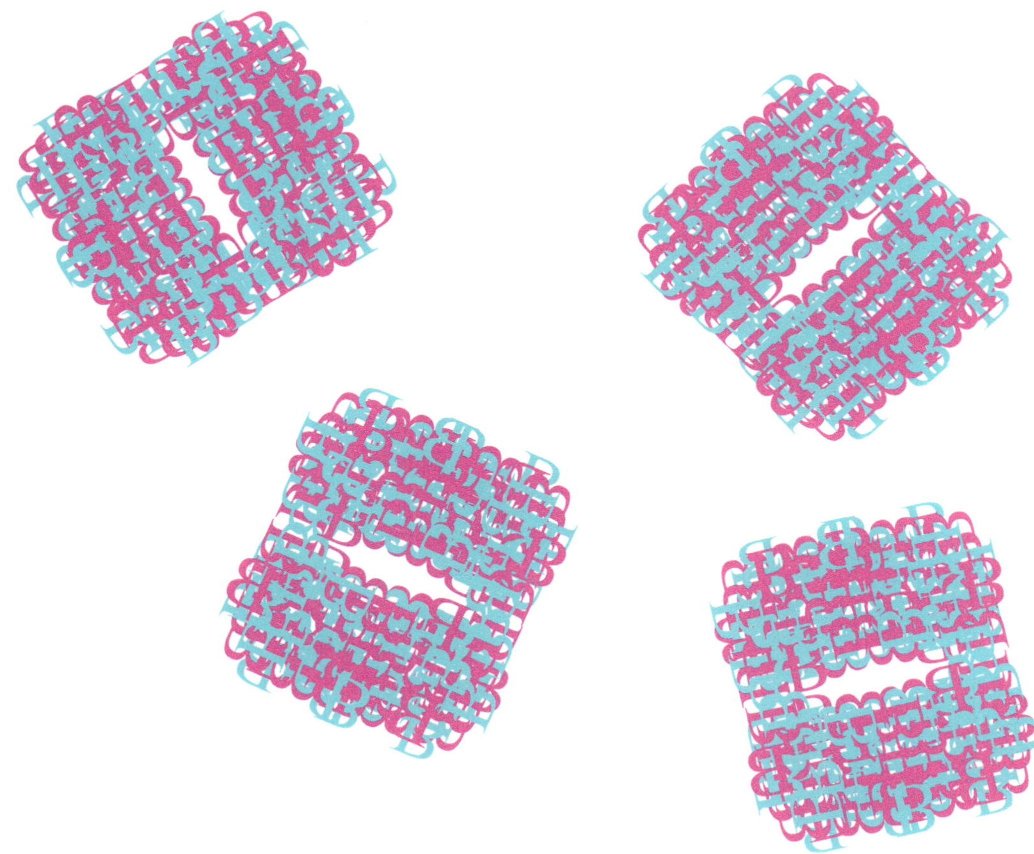

I think meaning is ambiguous. I make concrete objects that stay the same pretty much for the whole time they exist, and you can go away, and you can come back, and maybe you've changed, but the object will be the same.

—Ken Price, 2005

After *Carlo Scarpa Venini 1932-1947*

For Carlo Scarpa

In this period he searched for pure beauty trying to model a fluid material with the rigor of a clearly worked out project but the immediacy of the execution of Oriental calligraphy. He thus created several hundred unique pieces: forms blown by the unpredictable mastery of craftsmen, the joyous freedom in inventing decorations.

—Guido Pietropoli, "Carlo Scarpa's Hands." In Marino Barovier, *Carlo Scarpa Venini 1932-1947*

I

A Bollicine and Sommersi

H U

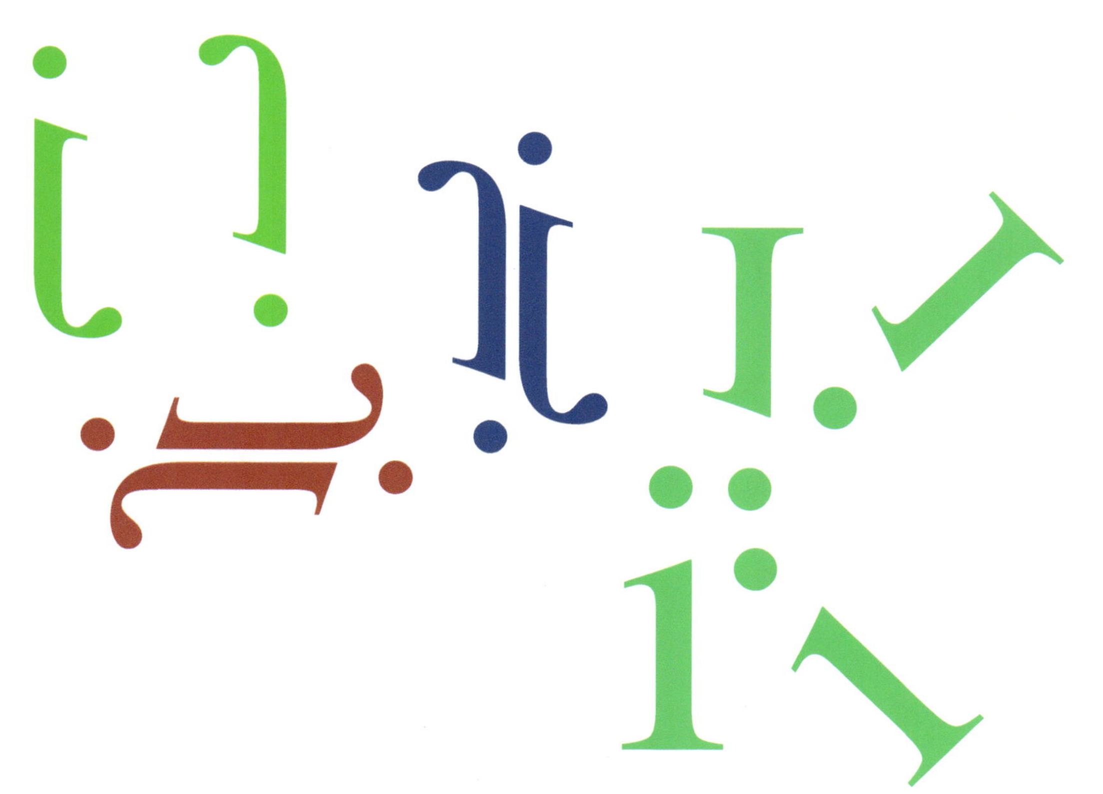

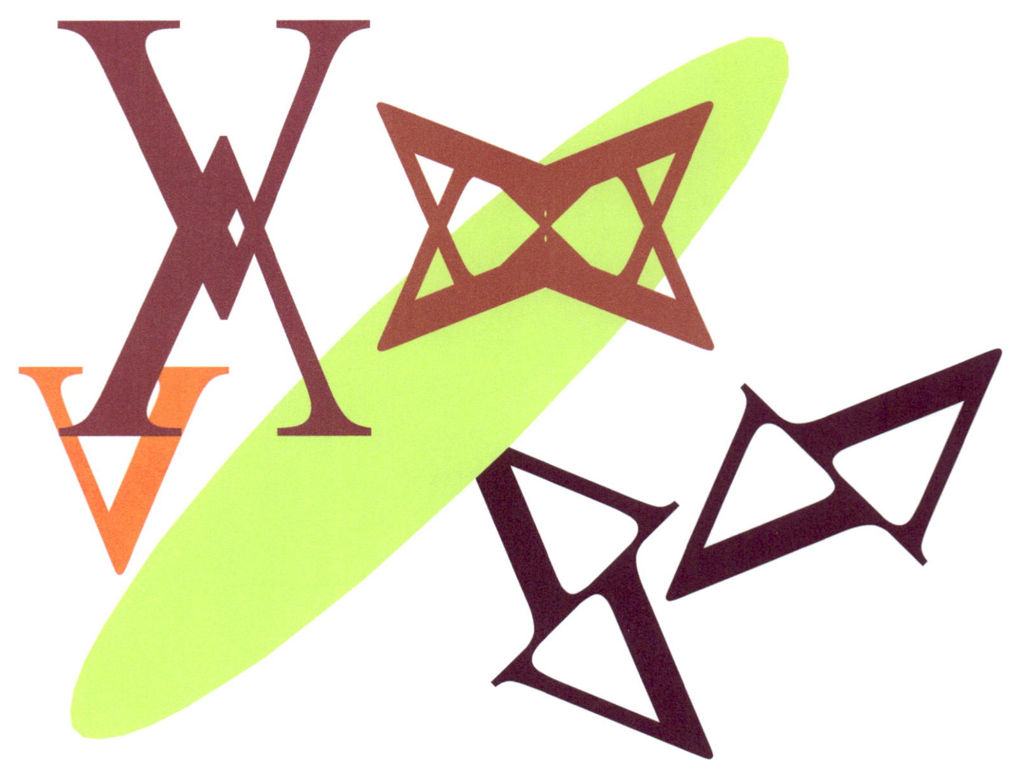

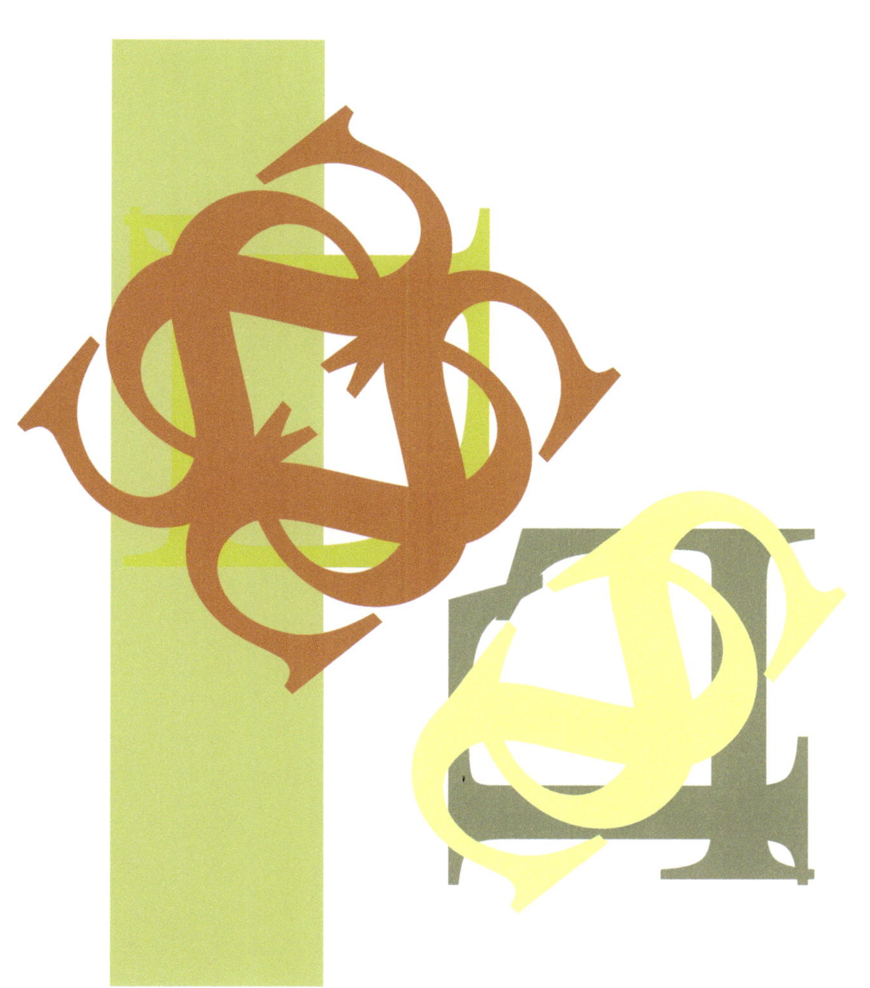

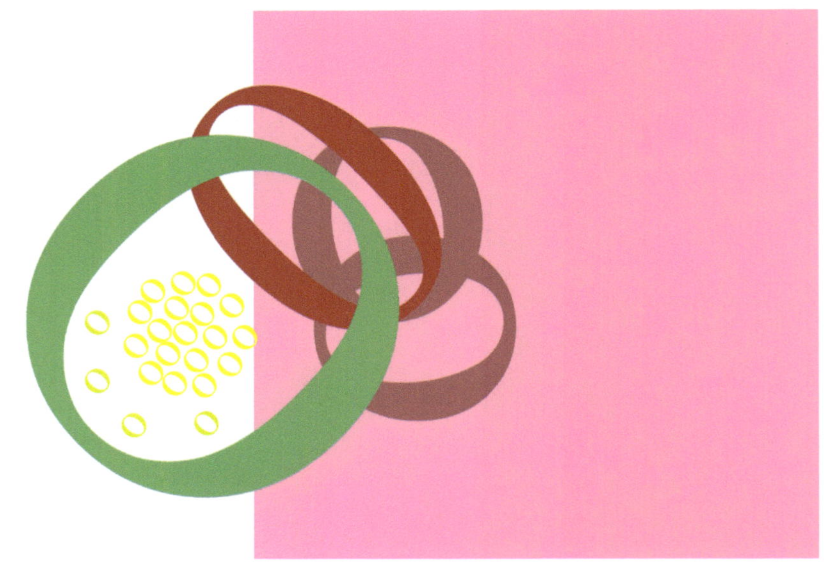

II

Incamiciata "Cinesi"

Je suis belle, ô mortels! comme un rêve de pierre,
Et mon   où chacun s'est meurtri tou   tour,
Est   pirer au poëte un am
F   si que la matière

                  comme un
                  ige à la bla
                  qui dépla
                  et jamais

                  es grandes
                  runter aux p
                  jours en d'aus

Ca   sciner ces dociles an
De puis   oirs qui font toutes choses pl   belles :
Mes yeux, mes larges yeux aux clartés éternelles!

haut dédiant leur onyx,
soutient, lampadophore,
îlé par le Phénix
cinéraire amphore

alon vide : nul ptyx,
é sonore
lé puis
dont

Mais proche la croisé
Agonise selon peut-é
Des licornes ruant d

funte nue en l
ns l'oubli ferm
ttillations sitôt le

La connais-tu, DAFNE, cette   enne romance,
Au pied du sycomore, ou sou   uriers blancs,
Sous l'olivier, le myrth   ou les   remblants,
Cette c   son d'   jo   mmer

Recon   tu le   PL   ristyle   e,
Et les   s   ù s'in   ient
Et la g   fat   hôtes   l
Où du   on va   rt l   e.

Ils rev   ce   pleur   urs
    ten   l'on   ancie
          re   un sou   ph

Ce   la sib   isa
Est e   e enc   C   in
— Et   é   portiq

mme un rêve d   suis belle, ô mo   s purs ongles tr   dédiant leur on
st meurtri tou   mon sein, où c   Angoisse ce mi   tient, lampado
été un amour   fait pour insp   nt rêve vespé   par le Phénix
matière.   ret et muet a   ne recueille   éraire ampho

un sphinx   ne dans l's   es crédence   vide : nul p
n blancheur   s un cœur c   i bibelot d'   re,
place les li   is le mouve   le maître   des pleur
ais je ne ri   ais je ne l   ce seul ob   néant s'hon

des attitude   oètes, deva   proche la   bord vacante
ux plus fie   j'ai l'air d'   sir selon p   écor
d'austères c   sumeront le   licornes rua   ontre une ni

Ses purs ongles très haut dédiant leur onyx,
L'Angoisse ce minuit, soutient, lampadophore,
Maint rêve vespéral brûlé par le Phénix
Que ne recueille pas de cinéraire amphore

Sur les créd… vide : nul ptyx,
Aboli bibel…
(Car le maî… es pleurs au Styx
Avec ce seu… ant s'honore.)

Mais proche la croisée au nord vacante, un or
Agonise selon peut-être le décor
… licornes ruant du feu contre une nixe,

… défunte nue en le miroir, encor
… ns l'oubli fermé par le cadre, se fixe
… illations sitôt le septuor.

Et la…
Où du dra…
Ils reviendront ces…
Le temps va ramener l…
La terre a tressailli d'un sou…
Cependant la sibylle au visage latin
Est endormie encor sous l'arc de Constantin
— Et rien n'a dérangé le sévère portique.

ancienne romance,
s les lauriers blancs,
es saules tremblants,
toujours recommence?

péristyle immense,
rimaient tes dents?
nprudents,
tique semence.

tu pleures toujours!
les anciens jours;
le prophétique…

… comme un rêve de pierre,
… s'est meurtri tour à tour,
… au poète un amour
… que la matière.

… r comme un sphinx incompris;
… e neige à la blancheur des cygnes;
… vement … les lignes,
… e ple…

… devan…
… l'air d'emp… iers monuments,
… eront leur jours en d'austères études;

… fasciner ces dociles amants,
… irs qui font toutes choses plus belles :
… es larges yeux aux clartés éternelles!

III

Corrosi

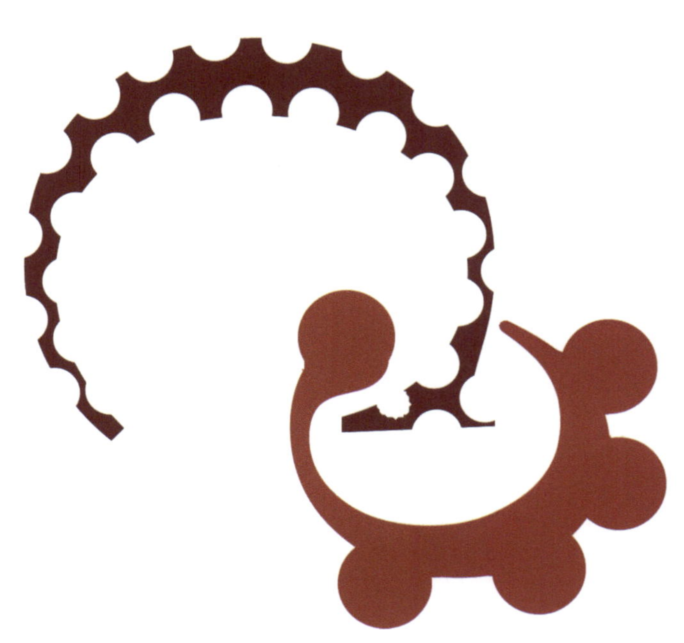

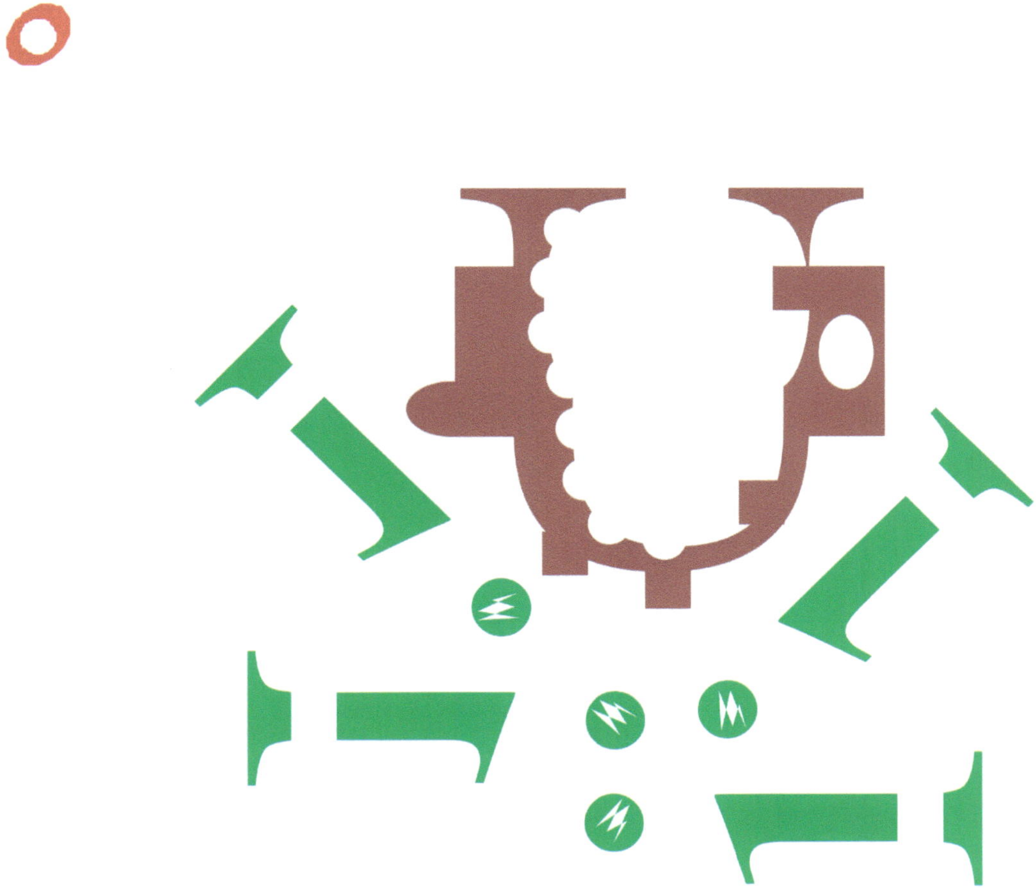

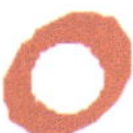

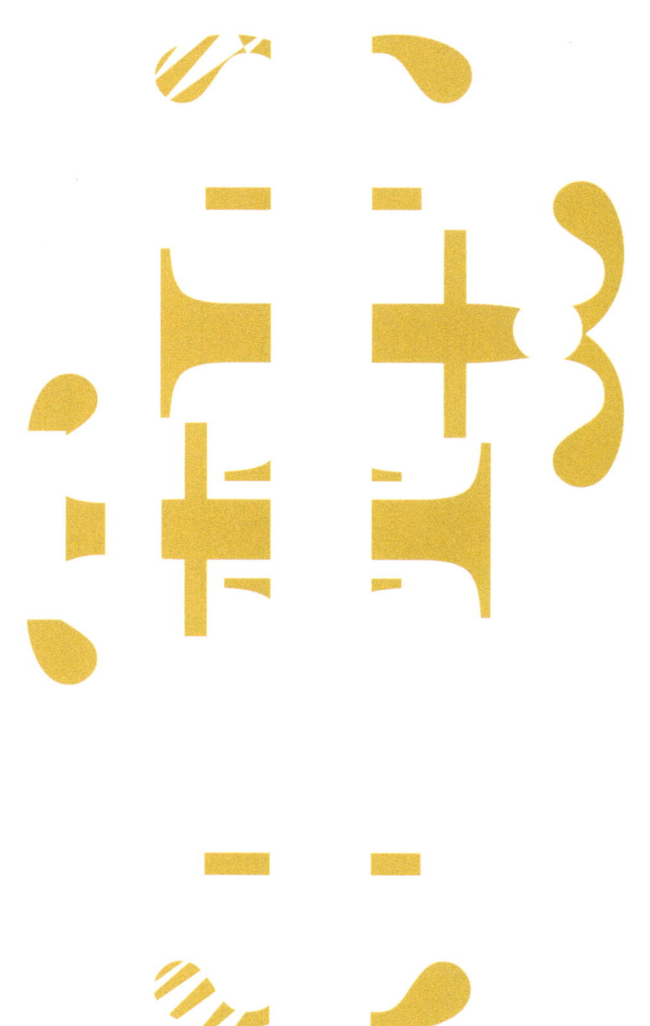

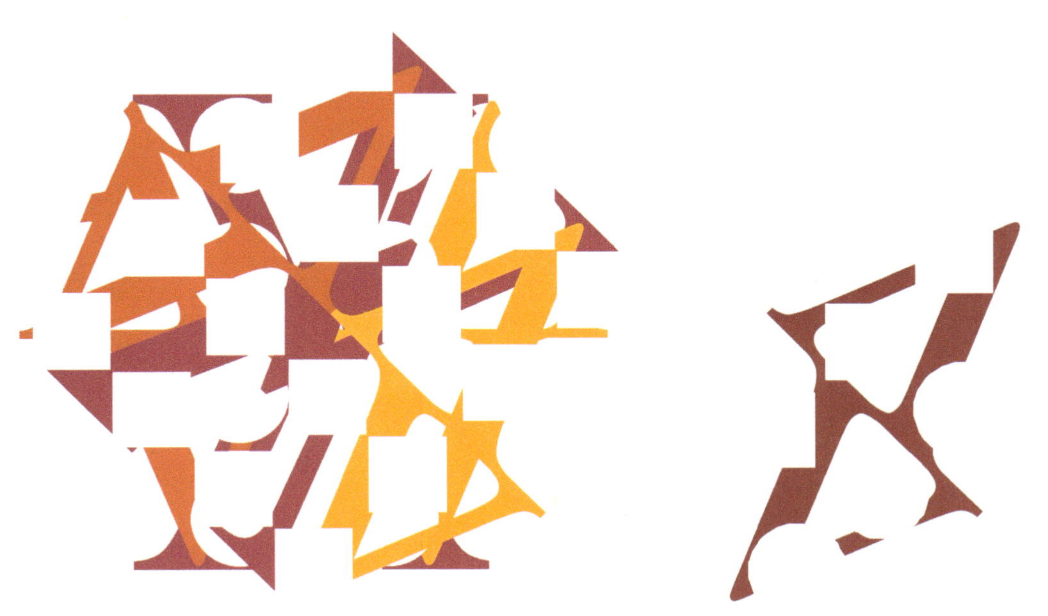

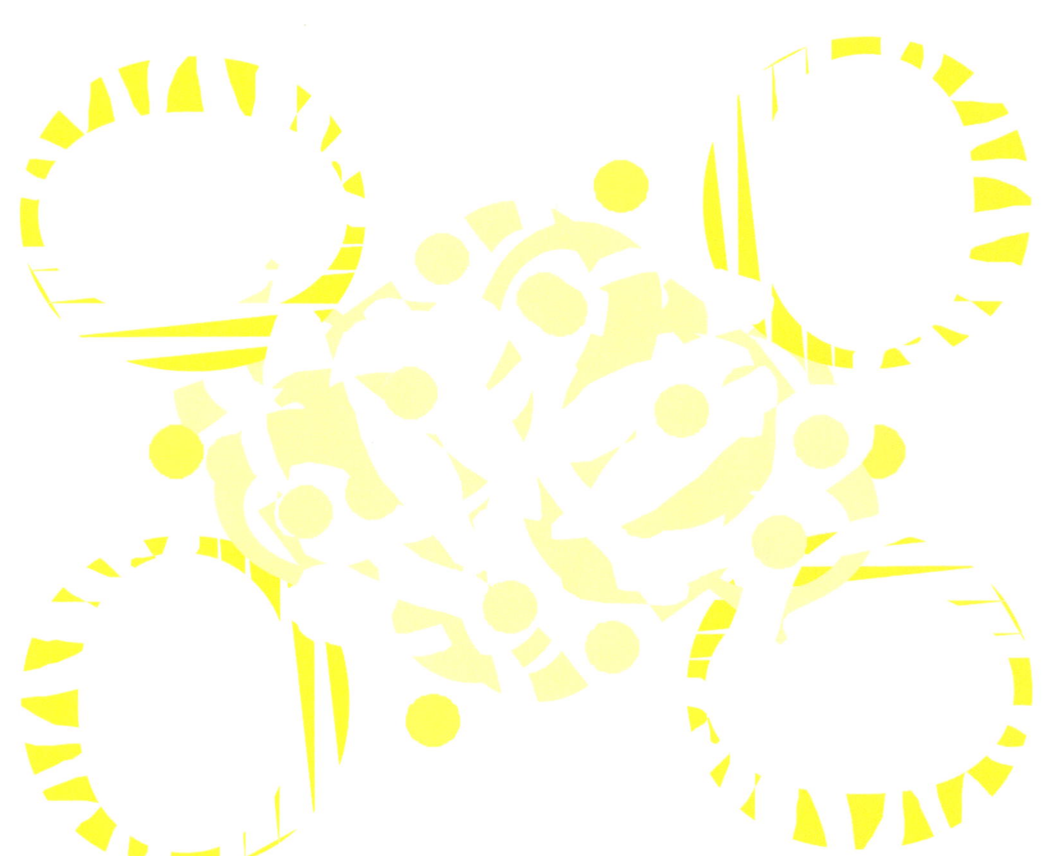

Trying to understand fully what he dealt with, recreating in his mind the sense of what the craftsman had tried to produce according to the unique and specific balance between form and matter, was both useful and playful for Scarpa.

—J. K. Mauro Piercontin, "Notes for a Chinese Cultural Scenario in the Glass and Work of Carlo Scarpa." In *Carlo Scarpa Venini 1932-1947*

After Anne Slacik

For Anne Slacik

parole

comme peinture — indémêlable, lorsqu'elle se prononce, de
la première aspérité.

—André du Bouchet, "aveuglément, peinture"

I

Mers

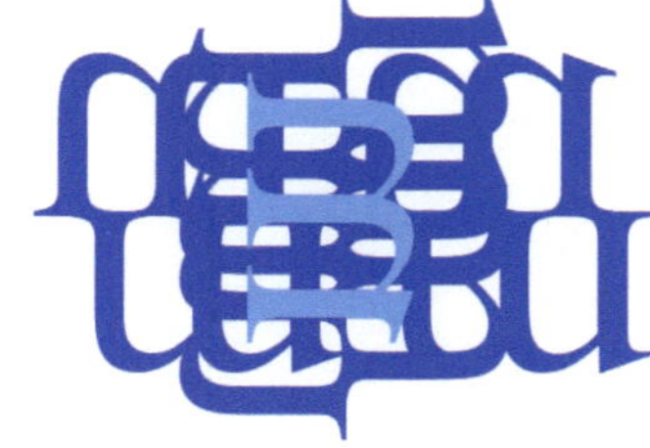

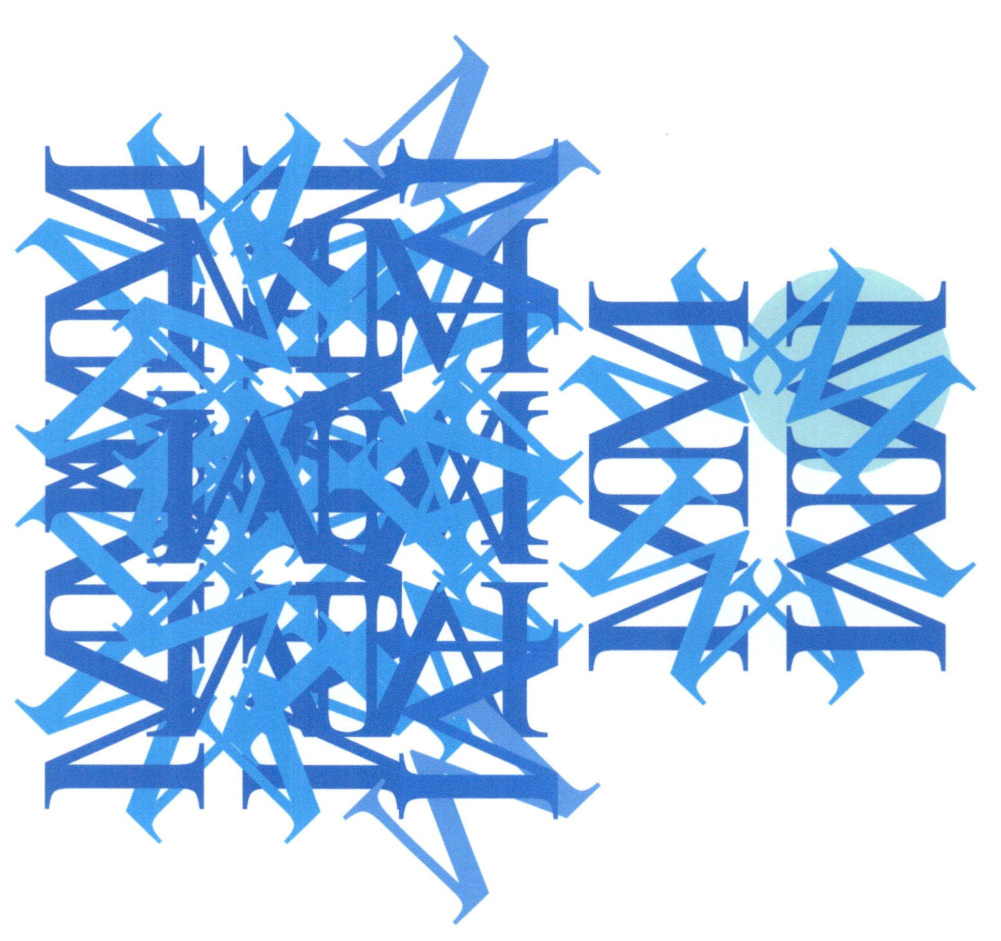

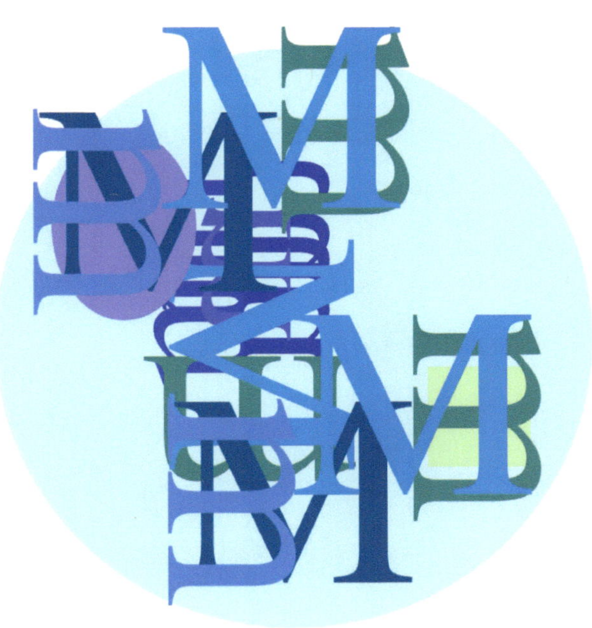

II

Danse Idéale

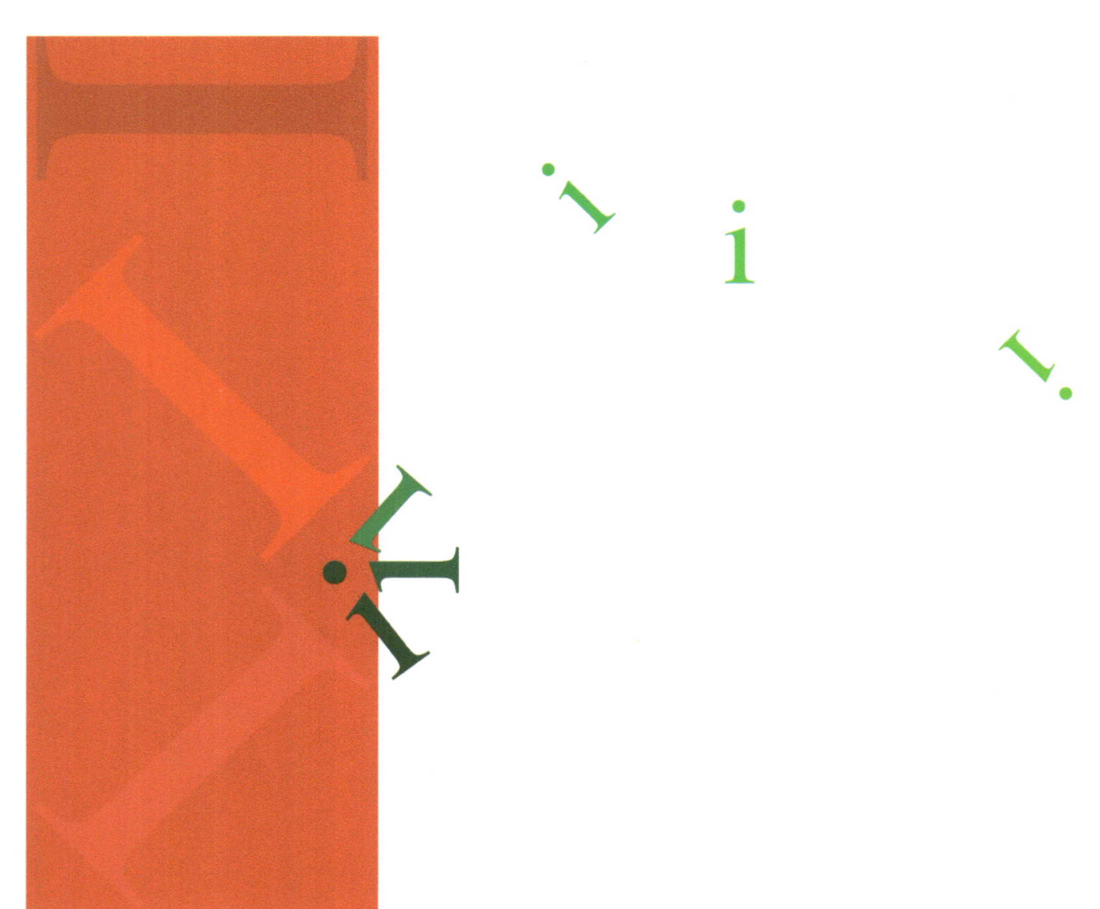

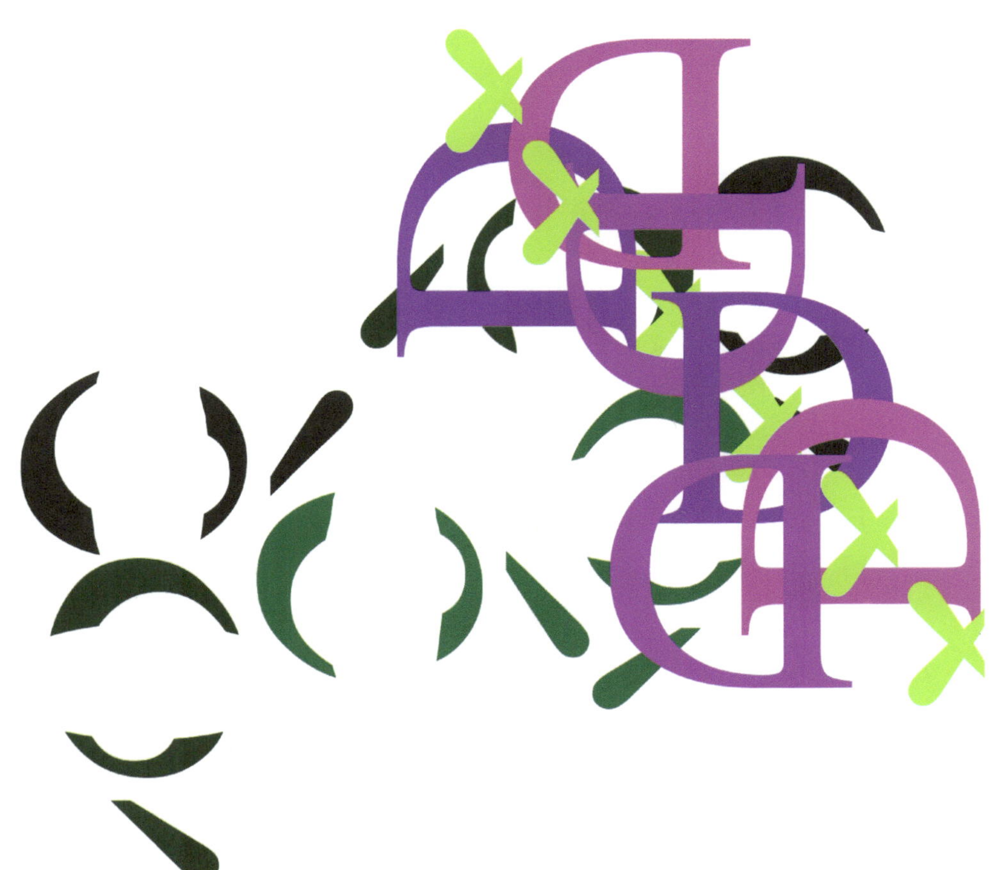

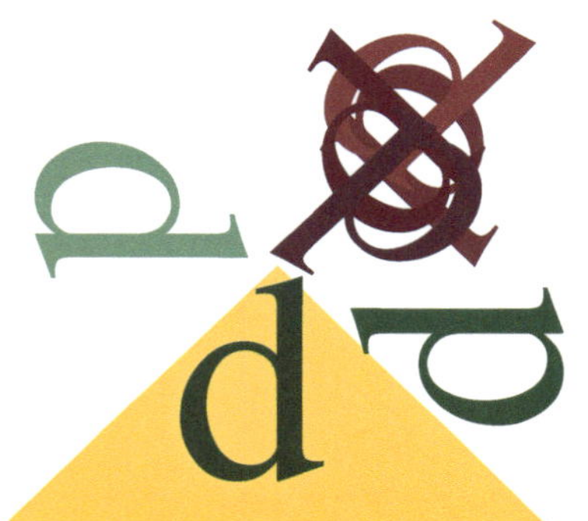

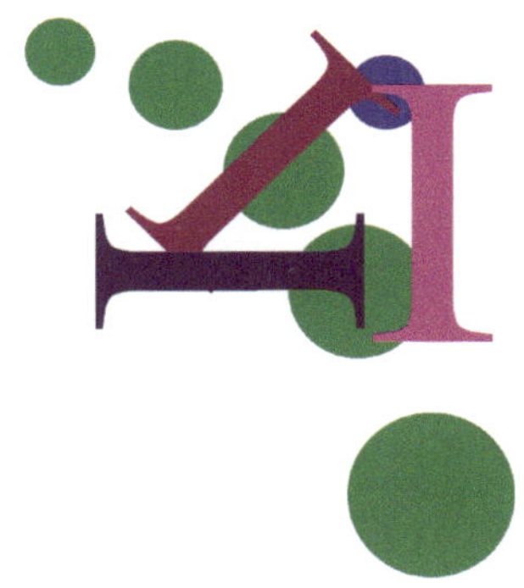
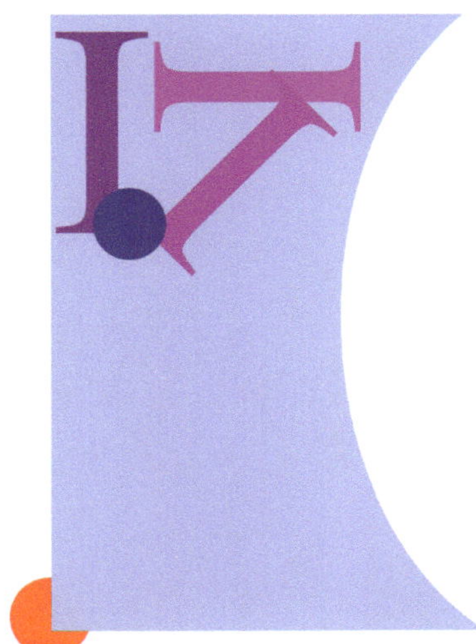

III

la langue elle-même : peinture (avec André)

la langue elle-même · peinture

le   ge

d'un m   au cond   r de la   eption p   entie —

commu   er sans   le se pe   ou qu'el   e soit pa   ule tout

à fait à   erdre —   itôt conf   u avec ce   aura été   u, dans

l'épaiss   lus avan   support.   à q   uiser.   comme

uyer.

peindre   contre   la   pa
demi-tour,   chemin   fai
                              de
du papier.
dans   notre   contenant
tour à tour, et le ciel —

i'aurai sur la rupture du
é   parole   à   l'épaisseur
nme à un mur s'attachera
            elle-même, la peinture,
tour à tour   —   terre

peinture.

e eux e rue intervalle
qui sépare de la peinture   c est la peinture.

[...] s'il a, recréé par lui-même, pris soin de conserver de son débarras strictement une piété aux vingt-quatre lettres comme elles se sont, par le miracle de l'infinité, fixées en quelque langue la sienne, puis un sens pour leurs symétries, action, reflet, jusqu'à une transfiguration en le terme surnaturel, qu'est le vers; il possède, ce civilisé édennique, au-dessus d'autre bien, l'élément de félicités, une doctrine en même temps qu'une contrée.

—Stéphane Mallarmé, "La Musique et les Lettres"

Notes & Translations

Disquiet

Epigraph from Richard Zenith's translation of *The Book of Disquie*t (Penguin, 2002).

After Mira Schendel

After the exhibition, *Tangled Alphabets: León Ferrari and Mira Schendel.* The Museum of Modern Art, New York, April 5th-June 15th 2009. All the epigraphs are statements by Schendel cited in the exhibition catalogue (The Museum of Modern Art, 2009). https://www.moma.org/calendar/exhibitions/299.

After *TILA (Doors)*

After the book of photographs, *Pertti Kekarainen Density TILA Series* (Photology, 2006). http://anhava.com/artists/pertti-kekarainen/.

Epigraph:

"I feel then the agreeable and difficult weakness of our writing—this with which it is also necessary to struggle and outwit oneself—that dreams always of pictograms, of ideograms, that would like to keep up in this vein, so thin with us, that makes of the gesture a writing and of all writing the manifestation of a corporeal presence."

Postgraph:

"Even if I sometimes dream of a writing so extreme that it can do without me, without words and without the thing. Gravitation of the poem in the anonymity of a sense washed by the slag of a vocable, of the trace of a flesh and of the anecdote of an object [...]."

Epigraph and postgraph from Nicolas Pesquès, *La face nord de Juliau, deux* [*The North Face of Juliau, two*] (André Dimanche, 1997).

After *Ken Price Sculpture: A Retrospective*
After the exhibition, *Ken Price Sculpture: A Retrospective*. The Metropolitan Museum of Art, New York, June 18th-September 22nd 2013.

Epigraph, postgraph and section titles are all from exhibition wall texts.

After *Carlo Scarpa Venini 1932-1947*
After the exhibition, *Venetian Glass by Carlo Scarpa: The Venini Company, 1932-1947*. The Metropolitan Museum of Art, New York, November 5th 2013-March 2nd 2014.

The section titles refer to the different glass-blowing techniques Scarpa had the Venini workshop use to produce his glassware.

The epigraph and the postgraph are from the exhibition catalogue, *Carlo Scarpa Venini 1932-1947* (Skira, 2013).

The altered sonnets in the second section are, in order, Charles Baudelaire "La beauté", Stéphane Mallarmé "Sonnet en –yx", and Gérard de Nerval "Delfica".

After Anne Slacik
After various paintings by the French artist Anne Slacik, including paintings inspired by poets Stéphane Mallarmé and André du Bouchet. The section titles are taken from some of Slacik's series titles. In English they are, in order, "Seas", "Ideal Dance", and "language itself: painting (with André [du Bouchet])". http://www.anneslacik.com/la-danse-ideale-des-con-stellations
http://www.anneslacik.com/lavril

The altered texts in the last section are all by André du Bouchet and come from *peinture [painting]* (Fata Morgana 1983) and "aveuglément, peinture" ["blindly, painting"] (in *Une tache* [A stain]. Fata Morgana, 1988).

Epigraph:

"speech like painting* — inextricable, when it is pronounced, from the first asperity."
André du Bouchet, "aveuglément, peinture".

* "peinture" in French can mean paint, a painting, or the art of painting more generally.

Postgraph:

"[...] if he has, recreated by himself, taken care to conserve from his relief strictly a piety for the twenty-four letters, as they have been, by the miracle of infinity, fixed in some language his own, then a sense for their symmetries, action, reflection, all the way to a transfiguration in the supernatural term, that is the poetic line; he possesses, this Edenic civilized person, above any other good, the element of felicities, a doctrine at the same time a land."

Stéphane Mallarmé, "La Musique et les Lettres" ["Music and Letters"], 1895.

About the Author

Michael Sohn grew up in the Massachusetts town that spawned "Mary Had a Little Lamb". He has lived in Chicago, a whole lifetime in New York City, and presently lives in Marseille with his wife. For too many years he taught Freshman Composition in NYC while working on his own poems, reading and writing about contemporary French poetry, and thinking about the relationship between text and image, the visual arts and poetry. He has published articles on French poets Stéphane Mallarmé (1842-1898) and André du Bouchet (1924-2001). He is currently writing, in French, a book of experimental and "shaped" prose, Contre [Against], about the French painter Pierre Tal Coat (1905-85), du Bouchet and the problem of writing painting.

Wet Cement Press Books

WetCementPress.com/shop

Ninso John High
*Without Dragons Even the Emperor
Would Be Lonely*
Ensos, Parables & Koans

Andrea Clark Libin
Orphan of the Moon
Notebook of a Girl in a Moscow Station

Thoreau Lovell
Wilson Wiley Variations
Poetry

Michelle Murphy
Synonym for Home
Poetry

Barbara Roether
Saraswati's Lament
Poetry

Anthony Schlagel
My Dog, Me
Novel

Michael Sohn
Still Forms
Visible Poetry

Brit Washburn
Notwithstanding
Poetry